GORILLA MINDSET

HOW TO CONTROL YOUR THOUGHTS AND EMOTIONS, IMPROVE YOUR HEALTH AND FITNESS, MAKE MORE MONEY AND LIVE LIFE ON YOUR TERMS

MIKE CERNOVICH

Copyright © 2015, 2016 Mike Cernovich

All rights reserved. This book or any portion thereof may not be reproduced or used in any manner whatsoever without the express written permission of the publisher except for the use of brief quotations in a book review.

Publishing services provided by:

ISBN-13: 978-1-5146-7211-2

WHAT OTHERS ARE SAYING ABOUT MIKE CERNOVICH'S MINDSET TECHNIQUES...

Mike Cernovich's mindset techniques have helped countless people improve their health and fitness, develop deeper personal and romantic relationships, and take control of anxiety and fear.

In *Gorilla Mindset*, you will learn how to:

- Improve your self-confidence by changing the way you talk to yourself and others.
- View the most brutal challenges as opportunities for personal growth with the power of reframing.
- Stop bad moods dead in their tracks and empower yourself to overcome obstacles, even when times are tough.
- Eliminate feelings of frenzy and absent mindedness.
- Develop quick, clear, and more focused thinking.
- Have a body that feels good and works for you, rather than against you.
- Earn more money by thinking of yourself as a personal brand.
- Live your life authentically.

Join the millions of people who have learned how to start believing in themselves by following the *Gorilla Mindset* principles today!

CONTENTS

INTRODUCTION
Change Your Mindset, Change Your Life 9

CHAPTER 1
Mindset and Conversation: The Power of Self-Talk 21

CHAPTER 2
Mindset and Choice: Change the Way You Perceive
Life's Challenges 33

CHAPTER 3
Mindset and Being in the Moment: How to Check
into Your Life 41

CHAPTER 4
Mindset and Mood: How to Control Your State of
Mind 61

CHAPTER 5
Mindset and Focus: How to Take Control of Your
Attention 69

CHAPTER 6
Mindset and Lifestyle: Change the Way You Live 83

CHAPTER 7
Mindset and the Body: Health and Fitness 97

CHAPTER 8
Mindset and Posture: How Posture Affects Your
Physical and Mental Health.. 129

CHAPTER 9
Mindset and Money: How to Keep Money in Perspective
and in Your Pocket... 141

CHAPTER 10
Mindset and Vision: Change What You See, Change
What You Get.. 167

CHAPTER 11
Mindset Starts Today: Creating Your Amazing Life
One Day at a Time... 173

WHAT'S NEXT?... 177

MORE INFORMATION

In addition to authoring Gorilla Mindset, Mike Cernovich is the producer and host of the most successful mindset podcast on iTunes. You can learn more about Mike, and obtain free supplemental reading and listening materials at GorillaMindset.com.

INTRODUCTION

CHANGE YOUR MINDSET, CHANGE YOUR LIFE

Gorilla Mindset is a book for those who want more out of life. That could mean taking control over your emotions, having a better relationship with your children, more money, better romance, a more rewarding career, or even freedom from anxiety and depression.

But there's a catch. To get more out of life, you must get more out of yourself. You must take personal responsibility for your thoughts and emotions. You must stop blaming the system. The days of looking outside of yourself for answers are gone!

This goes against what we've all been taught. We are told that the secret to getting more out of life is to buy some new gadget or car, or to drink beer or smoke cigarettes. One successful cigarette ad campaign proclaimed: *"You've come a long way, baby."*, as if inhaling cancer represented a triumph of women's liberation and the apex of human freedom.

All of us have tried filling the void with material objects. We see something bright and shiny. Maybe it's a new watch, car, or piece of jewelry. Something inside of us says we are lacking, and if we make this purchase, our need will be met.

That is a lie. To get more out of life, you must get more out of yourself. The hard work starts with you. Don't get me wrong, this is not a book of feel-good nothingness and validation. The work is hard, but also quite fulfilling.

This book teaches you how to get the most out of yourself. By the time you finish, you will be on your way to total control of your thoughts and emotions — the building blocks to life. You will get more out of life by getting more out of yourself.

Who Is Mike Cernovich:

You want to know why my book will work for you and, quite frankly, who the hell am I to tell you anything? Those are legitimate questions. This is a practical book on mindset. The techniques in the following chapters, while being backed by research, were first applied to my own life.

I grew up as a child on welfare. I had holes in my clothes. My parents, while good and well-meaning people, had no concept of how to make or save money. They made mistakes but did the best they could, which is all we can expect from anyone.

Not only was I usually the poorest kid in school, I was also the fattest. I was "naturally" chubby and got bullied a lot. I was afraid to walk home from school because kids would follow me, ridiculing me along the way, and then beat me up.

My dad told me to take martial arts, and he even started taking classes with me. I was not naturally athletic. I was clumsy and out of shape, I couldn't even do a single push-up. I hated martial arts classes and would have quit had my dad not been there. I went through the motions, but I had no natural talent or belief in myself.

One day a bully beat me up badly. It was humiliating. My sister had to pull my attacker off of me. I felt demoralized and powerless. We had a mattress in our garage, so I laid down there and cried myself to sleep. When my dad came home from work, he opened the garage door looked down at me, and with both pity and contemp, he asked me one question that changed my life:

"*When are you going to get serious?*"

Those words, coupled with the expression on his face, were a wake-up call for me. I made the decision right then and there to get serious. Very serious.

I would train until my body was exhausted and hit the heavy bag until my knuckles bled. I read in a martial arts magazine that Thai fighters do 10 rounds on the heavy bag, so I committed to do the same. When I learned that Thai boxers would roll up magazines and hit their shins to toughen themselves up, I did that as well.

I learned that when you consciously put in the work, you make progress. You may have terrible genetics, you may not have the potential to be in the Olympics or win a UFC title, but you *will* improve.

I earned my black belt in Tae Kwon Do, did boxing, and began beating up the bullies who had bullied me. I had a hair-trigger and would even look for reasons to fight. But I was never happy, and my social skills were poor. I felt awkward and weird. My mindset was based on vengeance, rather than exploration, connecting with people, and being happy.

At one point, I was invited to attend a school "lock-in" at the YMCA with a group of other classmates. I was so wrapped up in "fight mode" that I put on Tiger Balm to keep my joints warm, ready for someone to start a fight with me.

I also didn't perform well in school. Every teacher had the same line for my parents at PTA meetings: "*Michael is so smart, but he does not live up to his potential.*"

It wasn't that I enjoyed getting into trouble, but where I came from, getting good grades and doing homework wasn't the norm. I'd get into fights, steal sandwiches from the local grocery store, and shoot out car windows with a BB gun (which was stolen). When one of my acts of vandalism made the local newspaper, I clipped out the picture with pride.

To change my life, I had to change my mindset. The anger inside me had to be refocused into something less destructive and more productive. It took a lot of work, but I ended up going from a poor bullied fat kid without any money, to a well-known lawyer, writer, and podcast producer who travels the world. In many ways, my success makes me laugh, as my life story can seem unbelievable.

I'm still working hard at improving every day. Sometimes when people say they like me or ask me for advice, it's hard to understand why. There are days I still feel like the fat kid who was afraid to walk home from school. But here I am – successes, failures, and flaws – in all their shame and glory. That said, I think you'll find that I have some helpful advice to give. To begin, I want to ask you:

Are you ready to get serious?

What Is Mindset:

The online encyclopedia (that some people love, and many hate), *Wikipedia*, defines mindset as:

> *a set of assumptions, methods, or notations held by one or more people or groups of people that is so established that it creates a powerful incentive within these people or groups to continue to adopt or accept prior behaviors, choices, or tools.*

Imagine a computer. The monitor, keyboard, and processor are the hardware. Without any software to run it, your computer would be worthless. Your body is your hardware and your mindset is your operating system. It gives you access to the power of the hardware, and determines what software you can run. It lets you get the most out of your computer, allowing you to balance your checkbook and even create 3-D designs.

Your mindset determines how you perceive and interact with the world.

Mindset and the New Psychology of Success:

It was Carol Dweck who led the mindset revolution in her breakthrough book, *Mindset: The New Psychology of Success*. Dr. Dweck identified powerful research into psychology showing that the difference between success and failure often had less to do with innate talent, and more to do with the type of mindset one has: a growth mindset or a fixed mindset. Research showed that those who adopted a growth mindset — a belief that challenges in life present an opportunity to grow your abilities — were far more likely to succeed than those with a fixed mindset. That is, a belief that your intelligence and ability do not increase, but instead, have a set-point.

Dr. Dweck's work is invaluable, but is primarily a scholarly work, rather than one focused on application. In *Gorilla Mindset*, you will learn how to apply a growth mindset to your life. In addition, you will be introduced to the power of the abundance mindset.

Adopt an Abundance Mindset:

Just as mindset can be understood as being "growth" or "fixed," "abundance" and "scarcity" are polar mindsets present in life. Those who have an abundance mindset are far more likely to be happy with their lives and achieve their goals than those with scarcity mindset.

Imagine that you start with the assumption that we live in a world of limited possibilities. You have a fixed mindset, a belief you cannot change. You're limiting yourself. Nothing you do ultimately matters. You will never be good enough. If you begin with that scarcity mindset, why even get out of bed? Life would feel pointless. Nothing you do would matter. Life would be gray and empty. Many depressed people have a scarcity mindset, believing nothing matters and the world is one of limited possibilities.

Now, imagine you believe that the world is abundant. The world is one of endless resources and unlimited potential. What you do matters. Your choices matter. You matter. Each day is a new day full of infinite possibilities. How would you act if you knew that anything you wanted to do was possible? Would you live differently if you believed that you were abundant and full of potential?

Why *Gorilla Mindset* Is Different:

A gorilla is a powerful, dominant animal. We humans are known as "great apes" or "human primates."

Rather than view our physical nature as something dirty or evil, I embrace my gorilla nature. This doesn't mean being a mindless brute. This means recognizing that both mind and body are important for success and happiness. As you will learn in this book, mind and body are deeply connected. You cannot succeed in improving one without improving the other.

This book is about embracing your gorilla nature to find dominance and power, but you will see that this primarily means power over yourself, not others. The third eye in the gorilla recognizes we are great apes who seek enlightenment. We want answers. These answers cannot be found in our mind or body alone.

With *Gorilla Mindset*, you will recognize the power of unifying your body and mind — to simultaneously embrace and overcome your primitive nature.

Your Mindset Is A Choice:

Those of you who have children (or even a playful dog) are no doubt astounded they wake you up with excitement and curiosity. My dog wakes me up in the morning by jumping on my bed and licking my face. He acts as if he hasn't seen me in weeks and that our day presents endless excitement! To him, it's as if chasing a ball is something he has never done. My dog believes that each day offers unending possibility. In other words, my dog has an abundance mindset.

We all started off as children with an abundance mindset and genuine fascination and curiosity about life. Somewhere along the way, it was lost. Mindset is a choice. We can choose to view the world as one of scarcity or one of abundance.

Change Your Mindset, Change Your Life:

Remember the definition of mindset: "*a set of assumptions, methods, or notations," which are so powerful they force you to "continue to adopt or accept prior behaviors, choices, or tools.*" You can't change your life unless you change your mindset.

I've had more experience with this than most people. I thought there was no hope. I stopped looking at my environment and the people around me and started looking deep within myself. It was then that I learned a powerful secret.

The answer to all of life's most difficult questions resides within you. You may find that statement controversial now, but I promise that you won't once you finish this book. For several years, I have helped thousands of men change their lives through mindset training. Men have learned how to be more confident, assertive, and happier by changing their mindset.

But don't take my word for it. My podcast is one of the highest rated on iTunes and my websites have had millions of visits. Men across the world have written in and posted reviews like this:

> *"This podcast is mind bending. It will alter your consciousness into an alpha male godlike realm where anything is possible"*
> — Alex M.

> *"I can say with all honesty that Mike provides the most honest outlook on issues he is passionate about, that I have come across online."* — Sebastian

> *"If you want to improve yourself as a man, then this is the best podcast for you."* — P.N.

> *"Unfiltered, authentic, high-quality self-improvement."*
> — Rice S.

> *"Mike Cernovich's writing made me a better man. Period."* — Frank U.

No other "self-help" book has been targeted towards men like you. The message is always watered down to appeal to a wider audience. This book is for those of you willing to do whatever it takes to succeed. For those who are ready to get serious.

You Have Permission and the Tools You Need to Succeed:

When is the last time someone sat next to you and asked about your hopes and dreams? Society usually only speaks of duty and responsibilities, and loads you up like a pack mule. You're not allowed to seek danger, as that could jeopardize your ability to produce for this consumerist society. You're told not to seek play, as you need to be in bed early to wake up for some life you may not even want to live.

You're looking for permission and tools. I am giving you permission. As of right now, at this very moment, you are going to live life on *your* terms and be the one to define those terms. You already have the tools to do this, they are just locked up inside your mind. I'm going to give you the key to unlock your mind and live to your fullest potential.

This book is a key, nothing more.

The Gorilla Mindset System:

The heart of the Gorilla Mindset System is a paradigm that, when applied, will change how you think, feel, and live your life. In the first part of the book, we'll discuss the Gorilla Mindset Model. You'll start by mastering self-talk and then we'll move into reframing, mindfulness, mood, and focus.

Since mindset and lifestyle are connected, we'll also discuss some health, fitness, and other lifestyle changes you can make to improve your life. While each chapter stands on its own, they are especially powerful when approached in sync. The chapter on self-talk will lead into reframing, and both chapters will help you learn how to live in the present moment, which in turn, will improve your mood. You'll begin to see how your self-talk is influenced by how you choose to frame problems. As you work through the mindfulness and mood-control exercises, you'll begin to see how they can impact your health, confidence, willpower and much more.

Gorilla Mindset Shifts:

Throughout this book are immediate steps you can take to change the way you think titled, Gorrila Mindset Shift. These mindset shifts act as a "switch" in your brain. While they are subtle, you'll find they activate parts of your brain you havn't used in a long time, or perhaps, ever.

Gorilla Mindset Habits:

At the end of each chapter are actionable habits you can immediately apply to your life. These are small habits that will deliver big results.

Gorilla Mindset Worksheets:

In many cases, it's helpful to write out your patterns of thought. Where applicable, I've included worksheets you may use to further enhance your understanding of choosing and building your mindset. The Gorilla Mindset Shifts, habits, and worksheets, will help you not only understand, but apply your new mindset habits to your life. Now, it's time to change your life!

How to Use This Book:

This is a workbook, not a lecture. The operative word is *work*, and you will need to make a commitment to putting in the work, or reading this book will be a waste of your time. If you are ready to do the work, I have one request: Abuse this book. Print it out. Write on it. Annotate it. Scribble in it again and again, then throw it away and print out a new copy and do it again.

Writing is a physical act that engages your body and mind. Putting your words to paper makes your ideas real and concrete. It unites body and mind into one (as they *are* one). Take ownership of your life. Start by taking ownership of your words. These are exercises that I have performed and had thousands of other men perform. They work. They are based on science and personal experience.

Remember: This is *your* book, not mine.

Actively engage with this book. If you think I'm full of crap, great. Prove me wrong. Don't write to tell me I'm wrong, as your truth may be different from mine. Instead, focus on yourself and your goals: *"Mike is wrong. I'm not going to do what he suggests. I am going to do something else."*

The point is that you *do something*. If this book instills in you a sense that you must lead a more productive, more conscious life, then my job will be done. I'm here to share concepts and some specific examples from my own life. What will specifically work for you may differ from what works for me. Celebrate the difference.

Now, let's get to work!

CHAPTER 1

Mindset and Conversation: The Power of Self-Talk

"If you talked to your friends like you talk to yourself, you wouldn't have any friends."

— Mike Cernovich

Imagine that a friend of yours came to you for some advice. Perhaps he had lost his job or his wife left him. Imagine he was facing a real crisis and turned to you for help. What would happen to your relationship with this friend or loved one if your response was, "Your life is over!" You probably wouldn't have that friend for long, would you?

You should never candy-coat truths; but being overly dramatic is both inaccurate and unhelpful. Our friends turn to us for a combination of emotional support, validation, and actionable advice. You should support yourself in the same way.

GORILLA MINDSET SHIFT: TREAT YOURSELF LIKE A TREASURED AND TRUSTED FRIEND.

Think about how you talk to yourself when you are down. Here are some actual sentences I've uttered to myself:

- "You are so stupid!"
- "Why does this always happen to me?"
- "My life is over!"

While those negative sentiments are bad enough, what makes them worse is how overly dramatic they are. If you have said things like that to yourself, you know they have all proven to be false. Negative thoughts are usually lies. Besides, even if we do make a mistake, we can make a mindset shift to overcome the challenge.

Do you know anyone who has hysterical overreactions to everything in life, no matter how small? You probably try to avoid that person. Yet that is how we often talk to ourselves about our own problems. If talking to your friends like that isn't healthy, then why would talking to yourself like that be good for your mental health?

What Is Self-Talk:

Self-talk is the conversations you have with yourself. "Interlocution" and "intrapersonal communication" are two fancy ways of describing the same thing: the dialogue that runs through your head. Self-talk can be mundane, like repeating someone's telephone number that you're trying to remember; but it can also be a problem if you are in the habit of criticizing yourself.

Where We Learn Self-Talk:

We learned how to talk to ourselves from someone else. Unfortunately, the society we all grew up in is often negative. Even if our home lives were healthy and enriching (and many were not), we went to schools where people were bullied and small-minded people criticized and complained.

No one taught us how to talk to ourselves. It happened through osmosis. We silently repeated the same speaking patterns, words and phrases to ourselves that others had spoken to us. You could spend hundreds of hours on a therapist's couch analyzing where you learned how to talk to yourself. But where you learned it is not the question you need to answer. *Gorilla Mindset* is not about blaming your parents, teachers, other loved ones or authority figures. This is a book about taking action.

How to Improve Your Self-Talk:

There's a well-known marketing adage that applies in times of a brand crisis. Imagine your company or an employee is under attack. What can you do?

GORILLA MINDSET SHIFT: CHANGE THE CONVERSATION.

To improve your self-talk, the first step is to recognize that you're actually engaging in self-talk. This may seem obvious, but how many times has your mind "spiraled out of control?" When an internal conversation starts, seize it. (In Chapter 3 you'll be given specific techniques to help you get into the moment.) Write it down. Then look at the piece of paper so you can literally see the things you are saying to yourself. Once you've recognized that a conversation has started, take these four actionable steps to improve your self-talk:

1. Talk to Yourself in a Mirror

Rather than merely attacking yourself in silence, bring the conversation out of your head. Go look in the mirror. Begin talking. Do not censor yourself. Have the same conversation in front of the mirror that you were having inside your head. As you're talking, become observant. Look at your facial expressions. Does your brow furrow? Does your face look monstrous? That look you see in the mirror is what your unconscious mind sees when you talk yourself down. It is ugly, hateful, and disgusting. Ask yourself: Is this person looking at me, the person I want myself, my family, and my friends to see?

2. Record Those Nasty Voices

Get a tape recorder, or use your computer or iPhone's record function. In today's smartphone era, there are many simple ways for you to record yourself. Turn on the recorder and start talking. As with the mirror exercise above, do not censor yourself. Be real. Let it all out. Say all of those mean, nasty, angry thoughts out loud. Get it out of your system! Then, in a day or two, play back the recording. Listen to it objectively. You will realize it sounds ridiculous. When my coaching clients perform this exercise, they often feel disgusted. They simply cannot believe they said those things. Yet before using the recorder, my clients repeated those words to themselves day in and day out.

Save the recording. When your self-talk starts to become negative, play it to remind yourself of how ridiculous it really sounds. You'll probably want to delete it a day or two later. It will be embarrassing. You should feel free to delete it, after all, you are learning and growing and moving on with your life. But if you catch yourself trapped in negative self-talk again, make a new recording. Make as many recordings as you need to remind yourself what negative self-talk really sounds like.

3. Ask Yourself Questions

Criticism and self-hate are not based on open inquiry, they are based on value judgments. Most often, those value judgments were someone else's. The attacks in your head are other people's voices that you've heard and internalized over the years. That means that you are attacking yourself based on someone else's standards. How goofy is that?

Self-hate is not based on inquisitiveness. It is a rant: repeating negative statements over and over. When you feel yourself going on a self-destructive, self-hating rant, stop making statements and start asking questions:

- Am I being a hateful person?
- Do I want to be a hateful person?
- Am I a drama queen?
- Am I the type of person who loses my mind over stupidity and nonsense?
- Am I choosing, in this moment, to be the type of person I want to become?

Ask those questions. Answer them. Literally start a new conversation. As you ask more questions, a rich conversation will emerge. You'll begin to reconsider your assumptions about the world. You may even begin asking the most fundamental questions of all:

- Who am I really living for?
- Who do I want to be?

4. Affirmations and Mantras

Change negative self-talk into positive self-talk. Positive self-talk can come in the form of affirmations or mantras. An affirmation can be a sentence, paragraph, or even a full page of conversation you have with yourself. A mantra tends to be shorter, usually a word or two. When writing your mantra, imagine the person you want to be. Visualize it. (In Chapter 10, you'll learn exactly how to do this.) Repeat your affirmation or mantra as often as you need to. Many people begin their days with one or both, and others use them when under stress.

Here are some examples:

- "I am unstoppable."
- "I love the smell of Napalm in the morning. It smells like victory." [From *Apocalypse Now*.]
- "This is a fantastic challenge that will test my resolve and will. Even if I don't win, I will grow stronger."
- "Today I am better than I was yesterday." [From *Last of the Renshai*, a science fiction book.]
- "The only easy day was yesterday." [Navy SEAL motto.]

I knew a doctor who, when confronted with a problem would say, "*Mighty.*" By repeating, "*Mighty! Mighty! Mighty! Mighty!*" he'd remind himself who he was. Again, it doesn't matter what your affirmation or mantra is. It's yours. There are no right or wrong answers. I want you to discover YOUR truth, not my truth. What matters is how you feel. Your mantra or affirmation should encourage, motivate, and in times of stress, comfort you.

GORILLA MINDSET SHIFT: IT'S YOUR AFFIRMATION. IT CAN BE AS "CORNY" AS YOU WANT IT TO BE. WHAT MATTERS IS THAT THE POWERFUL SELF-TALK RESONATES WITH YOU. YOU HAVE PERMISSION TO DO ANY GOOFY NEW AGE STUFF YOU LIKE, SO LONG AS IT WORKS.

Your mantra can be a short snippet of a full affirmation, and can even be a stepping off point for an entire code of conduct or creed. The United States Army Rangers, an elite special operations force that conducts some of the most dangerous missions around the world, makes each soldier memorize the Ranger Creed.

By being forced to memorize the creed, Rangers begin to live the creed. It includes some affirmations such as:

> *Never shall I fail my comrades. I will always keep myself mentally alert, physically strong, and morally straight and I will shoulder more than my share of the task whatever it may be, one-hundred percent and then some.*

That's powerful living!

Improving Your Self-Talk Will Improve Your Relationships:

Your self-talk affects your relationship with yourself. If you are constantly beating yourself up or using abusive language on yourself, you will be in a poor mood. You'll be angry, and no fun to be around.

Once you improve your self-talk, your mood will improve. What's more, your improved self-talk will have another effect: it will improve how you treat those around you. When you start talking more politely to yourself, your friends, family, business associates, and other loved ones may be surprised by how you are now talking to them as well.

You'll begin to choose your words more carefully. When you stop insulting and overreacting to yourself, you will discover that you also don't overreact when dealing with others.

Create Powerful Affirmations:

Extensive research into the science of willpower and mindset has shown that people are far more likely to believe something when they are given a reason to do so. Unless you have a reason for your affirmation, you may not believe in it, and you won't follow through.

Your affirmation can be anything from a belief you hold about yourself, to a commitment to engage in a new task or set of habits. In other words, "affirmation" is not a fundamental concept with a fixed meaning. It is not a rule to abide by, or a clever saying. It is an action or a process of encouragement. Structure your affirmations as follows:

- I am going to _____, because _____.

For example:

- I am going to warm-up my brain before work because I enjoy having clarity of thought and intense focus.
- I am going to take a contrast shower because I want to feel invigorated.
- I am going to get out of bed rather than hit the snooze button because I'm tired of being passive about life.

Write or type out your affirmations on a piece of paper. Your affirmation can be short or long. For example, the following essay, "*I Will*", is my affirmation on life:

I WILL

Maybe this, maybe that, maybe I'll be a contender.

Mr. Maybe is the ultimate seducer. Mr. Maybe whispers honey in your ear.

When you talk to Mr. Maybe, he tells you what your ego wants to hear.

Maybe gives you the illusion that someday, by golly, you'll live the life you dreamed of. Mr. Maybe tells you, "It will happen. Trust me!"

Committing to Mr. Maybe is easy. It requires no risk, only rationalization.

"I could have been a contender," you'll tell yourself later in life when you inevitably realize that the only certainly that follows maybe is regret.

Don't "Call me maybe?"

There is no maybe. There is no "I might."

There is no, "That sounds interesting. Maybe I'll do it one day."

You are in, or you are out.

There is only the daily, hourly, minute-by-minute, unrelenting commitment.

Make a commitment to yourself, starting this very moment.

It's a basic commitment that only requires two words: I will.

- I will treat today like the beginning of a new life.
- I will go to the gym.
- I will turn off the television.
- I will stop reading filth, rage, and click-bait websites.
- I will fuel my body for optimal performance.
- I will make more money than I spend.
- I will visualize my perfect day.
- I will keep moving, fighting, striving and giving the world my all.
- I will fall asleep a better man than I woke up.

Are you willing to kill Mr. Maybe?

You're either in or you're out.

What it's going to be?

THE SELF-TALK WORKSHEET:

Self-talk refers to the conversation we have with ourselves. To improve the conversation with yourself, put your words into writing. Filling out this worksheet will help you become more mindful of your language and thought patterns.

How to Speak to Yourself:

What words and phrases do you use when talking to yourself? What is the phrase you most commonly use when you find yourself in a troubling situation?

Write it out: _____

Here's an example from my own life: I tend to speak in absolutes. When something doesn't go my way or when I make a mistake, I say to myself, "*You always mess this up,*" or "*You never get this right.*" This negative thinking reinforces an unconscious belief that I am incompetent. It is harmful and destructive.

When you talk to yourself in that way, how do you feel?

Write it out: _____

Example: I tend to feel hopeless, as I am always making the same mistakes or feel like I can never do anything right. Using words like "never" or "always" make me feel like growth or change is impossible.

What is an empowering or comforting phrase you can use when talking to yourself?

This must be a phrase that YOU own. When you make a mistake, how can you recognize and make a correction without beating yourself up?

Write it out: _____

Example: I often make mistakes. My mistakes are not an indictment of my character but a reminder that I am human. Each mistake gives me an opportunity to reflect and grow.

Better Self-Talk Will Lead to Better Conversations with Others:

As you perform those self-talk exercises, you'll notice a surprising side effect. You will start talking to your friends, family members, lovers, and others with a more helpful, encouraging tone. After all, much of the negative energy you direct outward, originates within yourself.

GORILLA SELF-TALK HABITS

1. Avoid Speaking in Absolutes

Rather than saying, "I always make this same mistake," recognize that each mistake is an opportunity for growth. Moreover, do you really "always" make the same mistake? That is probably not true and telling yourself you "always" make that mistake and will "never" improve is certainly not helpful. Instead say, "I made a mistake. I will avoid it in the future by _____."

2. Talk to Yourself as You Would a Close Friend

When going on a negative rant against yourself, stop and ask: "Would I talk to a close friend or loved one like this?" Maybe you would, but I doubt it. You are probably meaner to yourself than you are to others.

3. Smile When You're Angry at Yourself

Mood and posture are linked, and it's been proven that engaging in the physical act of smiling can actually make you feel happier. When you start talking to yourself in a negative manner, raise your body up, take a deep breath, and smile. You might find the rant stops in its tracks.

4. Turn a Critical Statement about Yourself into a Question

Rather than blame and talk down to yourself, ask, "How can I prevent making this same choice in the future?"

5. Talk to Yourself in Front of a Mirror

Look in the mirror as you talk to yourself. Repeat the same negative words to your face. How do you look? Is that the type of person you want to be?

6. Repeat Your Mantra

Your mantra or affirmations could be a word, a sentence, or even an entire essay.

CHAPTER 2

Mindset and Choice: Change the Way You Perceive Life's Challenges

We've all heard the expression, "It's all about your frame of mind." That is one of those pieces of homespun wisdom that everyone assumes you understand, but no one ever explains. We are left with an intuitive sense that some nebulous concept of "framing" exists and is important. But when you start to think deeply about what a frame is, it renders endless possibilities.

What Is Framing:

The idea that "frame of mind" is a form of mood makes sense in some ways, but there's a more powerful way of understanding what framing is, how it affects your life, and how you can change it.

As a lawyer, I learned a more technical meaning for the idea of framing. When lawyers speak of framing, they are talking about the key issue or legal question that matters in a case. That is, what question do you ask a judge or jury to decide?

How you ask a question and what facts you include when asking your question often influences the answer. This is "framing" your question. There are entire books devoted to "how to ask the right questions" when seeking a raise in salary, a favor from a friend, or even a date.

The way you ask a question can often determine how the question is answered. This is something even children understand. When they ask one parent for a privilege, they often frame the question as, "Mom said I could stay the night at my friend's house. Is that OK with you?" By including the fact that "mom said it's OK," the child is letting you know your answer won't cause drama or conflict. Even children know how to frame the issue!

Framing the issue is so important that entire chapters of legal books are devoted to framing exercises. Framing the issue involves choosing what facts you want the judge or jury to focus on. After all, life is messy. Not every fact matters. Some facts are material and some are immaterial.

Psychologists also use the idea of framing when studying preferences, choices, and risks. Any choice can be described in terms of its outcomes, both good and bad. Whether a decision is made using a positive frame (focusing on good outcomes) or a negative frame (focusing on bad outcomes) will radically change not only your decisions, but your willingness to take risks, and even the way you remember your decisions.

Framing is a part of our everyday lives. In the real world, decisions are complicated and problems are messy. We're somewhat moral, somewhat immoral, and somewhat confused. Some facts help us and some facts hurt us. Whether we are conscious of it or not, we constantly create frames for the stories we tell ourselves, and for the stories we tell other people.

Why Framing Matters:

In the Chapter Two, we looked at self-talk. When you talk to yourself, you're ultimately sending signals to yourself to control how you think and feel, and you understand how important those conversations are.

Imagine your consciousness is the judge or jury, or parent or friend that you must persuade. You want your conscious mind to believe in you. Framing is how your mind perceives whatever situation you are in. Framing is how you choose to think about, and thus perceive, a challenge in your life.

Framing Is How You Talk to Yourself:

The language you use impacts your frame. Are you facing a problem or a challenge? What language do you use?

A problem is merely something needing to be solved. You become more resourceful every time you discover a new solution. Truthfully, a problem can be perceived as an obstacle, or an opportunity. How you perceive it is a choice you get to make in the present moment by framing the issue.

Your Frame Is Your Focus:

Tony Robbins, a wildly successful self-help author, often says, "What you focus on is what you feel." Robbins is recognizing that how you frame an issue (i.e. what you choose to focus on) will determine how you feel about the issue. There is considerable scientific research on this topic. Let's start by asking a question: Would you rather win a silver medal in the Olympics or a bronze medal?

That's not a trick question. Would you rather finish in second or third place?

The answer may seem obvious to you. While a gold medal is best, why wouldn't you want to win a silver medal instead of a bronze medal. Yet research by Doctors Victoria Medvec, Thomas Gilovic, and Scott Madey, shows our intuitive answer is incorrect. We would actually be happier in the long run by finishing in third place!

In their study, "*When Less is More: Counterfactual Thinking and Satisfaction among Olympic Medalists*", Medvec and her colleagues examined the reactions and post-game statements of Olympic silver and bronze medalists from the 1992 Olympic games, and interviewed over one hundred and fifty silver and bronze medalists from the 1994 Empire State Games, to assess their state of mind. In both cases, the bronze medal winners both appeared happier and more satisfied during post-game interviews than the silver medal winners.

How could you not be happier with a silver medal than with a bronze medal? The answer lies in our focus. What do Olympic winners focus on?

- "I might have won a gold medal and been on a Wheaties box," says the silver medalist.
- "I might have not been on the podium at all," says the bronze medalist.

It's all in the frame.

The silver medalist chose to focus on what might have been (a gold medal). The bronze medalist also chose to focus on what might have been (no medal at all)! The silver medalist, rather than choosing to focus on how he almost became the next Michael Phelps, could instead reframe the issue, choosing to be grateful that he's even on the podium at all.

Always remember that your frame is a choice. How you choose to view life's difficulties and what you choose to focus on is a choice you make in the present moment.

GORILLA MINDSET SHIFT: REFRAME THE ISSUES. CHOOSE TO FOCUS ON HOW THE DIFFICULTY YOU'RE FACING WILL MAKE YOU STRONGER, MORE INTELLIGENT, MORE EMOTIONALLY COMPLEX, OR MORE RESOURCEFUL.

He Who Controls the Frame Controls the Debate:

There are several specific ways you can change your frame of mind. Reframe your problem as being small, relative to a worse problem. It's helpful to get out of your head, or as you may have heard growing up: "Get over yourself." Someone else has it worse. Look around. Express gratitude and choose to focus on what you have, rather than what you don't have.

Frame your problems as a source of power. Each problem you face is preparation for your big moment! What if, instead of feeling hopelessness or self-pity, you reframed your problem in this way:

"Once I've gotten through this problem, I will have a reservoir of strength that will make me unstoppable!"

Sure, you'll still have the same "problem." Yet, what happens to your mind and your body when you change how you think about this problem? Your breathing improves. Your posture is more upright. You no longer feel defeated. You develop a sense of, "Yeah, I got this." Remember that your mind and body are connected. When your frame is positive, you will feel stronger and more energetic as well. You embrace the struggle. "Yes, this hurts and is hard, but once it's over, no one will be able to stop me."

Framing Begins with a Choice:

Philosophers might debate about free will; but when you live your life day to day, you always have a choice. You can choose how you feel by choosing how you frame your problems. You can choose to view them as special and unique, the biggest burden in the world, or you can view your problems as being nothing compared to what others have endured. You can choose to view your problems as pointless suffering, or you can choose to view your problems as preparation for life. The choice is always yours.

THE FRAME CONTROL WORKSHEET:

What is your biggest problem? This could concern your health and fitness, finances, or relationships.

Write it out: _____.

Now, how can you reframe your problem as a challenge? For example, I might say, "My biggest problem is learning how to stick to a budget." I could reframe that problem into a challenge by saying, "I am going to learn how to track my spending in a software program like Mint."

What is one area of your life that can be improved by choosing to frame this problem as an opportunity for growth?

Write it out: _____.

List three ways solving your problem will help you grow:

1. _____,
2. _____,
3. _____.

If you're stuck, here are some ideas:

- Solving problems makes us more resourceful, which gives us more tools to succeed in life.
- Solving problems also requires self-discipline, which we could all benefit from.
- Finally, you will become more thoughtful and conscious by identifying challenges and opportunities in your life.

Could you choose to reframe your problems as being smaller, relative to other problems? For example, the silver medalist in the Olympics sees his problem as having not won the gold medal, whereas the bronze medalist feels lucky, as not winning a medal at all would have been a worse outcome.

Write out your problems and reflect on how much worse your life could be. This will give you a sense of gratitude for what you have.

GORILLA FRAME CONTROL HABITS

1. Watch Your Language

Instead of calling something a "problem," reframe it as a "challenge." That seems cliché, but it really works.

2. Remember That Growth Can Be Painful

Adopting a growth mindset is bittersweet. The bitterness comes from the pain accompanying growth. "No pain, no gain" is true. The sweetness comes from growth. Nothing feels as good as winning.

3. Remember That Pain Is Inevitable

Even if you didn't embrace the pain of growth, life would bring pain to you eventually. You cannot choose whether the pain is coming. As is said in Game of Thrones, a hit book series and later, an HBO adaption, "Winter is coming." Once you accept that pain is inevitable and leads to growth, you'll be better prepared to endure winter.

4. Take the Long View

The challenges you face today will give you the resources you need to succeed tomorrow. You fell down a lot as an infant before you learned to walk. You tripped when learning to run. At some point, you were clueless and made mistakes, yet those mistakes eventually led to your success and mastery.

5. Embrace the Suck

Let's face it. Sometimes life is going to be hard, and no amount of arguing or wishing it were otherwise will change that. When you go through hard times (and we all do), accept it and then embrace it. Army Rangers call this, "Embrace the suck." Rangers go through rigourous training and for 58 days they average less than 2 hours of sleep each night. Every day is worse than the last. Bodies ache and begin to break down. If they sat around complaining, they'd never get through it. Instead, they choose to "Embrace the suck," which allows them to endure and succeed.

CHAPTER 3

Mindset and Being in the Moment: How to Check into Your Life

We've covered a lot of ground in a short period of time. The concepts we are learning and applying to ourselves do not take a million words to explain. But the concepts are deep, and real understanding takes place only after taking action and applying these principles to your life.

We started off with self-talk, and then the power of choices, framing, and focus. Now you are ready to learn about mindfulness, and how getting into the present moment can give you freedom from anxiety and fear. Some think of "mindfulness" as esoteric or abstract, but you will see that it simply brings together all the ideas we have covered so far, and will have real practical consequences for your life.

What Is Mindfulness:

It's helpful to look at the definition others use so that we can see how our exercises build on, and sometimes deviate from, the common understanding of mindfulness.

Wikipedia defines Mindfulness as:

> *'the intentional, accepting and non-judgmental focus of one's attention on the emotions, thoughts and sensations occurring in the present moment,' which can be trained by meditational practices.*

That's a nice start, but does that definition clarify the concept for you? It doesn't for me. I have been applying mindfulness to my own life for more than 15 years, and still that dictionary definition tells me nothing applicable. It is too vague to be of any practical value. To understand mindfulness better, let's start with something more concrete. Sometimes it's helpful to think of the opposite of a concept in order to appreciate the concept. We all understand what it means to be mindless: in a lower state of consciousness, distracted, and unaware.

Mindfulness is the opposite of mindlessness. Mindfulness is a state of higher consciousness.

How I View Mindfulness:

- Mindfulness is freedom from anxiety or fear.
- Mindfulness is perception, not judgment.
- Mindfulness is getting out of your head and into your body.
- Mindfulness is checking in to the present moment.
- Mindfulness is being in the zone or in flow state.
- Mindfulness is being present and engaged.
- Mindfulness is being, rather than doing.

Your view of mindfulness may differ, and that's totally cool. I didn't write this book to prove anyone wrong. This book is for you to apply to your own life. The answers are already within you, and all we need to do is work through your issues to help you discover these answers. By the end of this chapter, you should have your own list of what mindfulness means for you. Whether that list is the same as mine or different, the goal of this chapter will have been achieved.

Now that we have a working definition of mindfulness, let's get to the fun part. The rest of this chapter is divided into two major sections. First, we will go through specific things you can do to become more mindful. Second, we will look at specific ways that your increased mindfulness can be used to change your mood, well-being, and effectiveness in life.

PART 1: HOW TO BECOME MORE MINDFUL

The dictionary definition mentioned meditation, so I'd like to start with this question: Is meditation necessary to become more mindful, present, aware, active, engaged, and checked-in?

Meditation is one approach that people can use to become more mindful. Indeed, in my teens and early twenties I trained with a master of Samadhi meditation. Meditation is valuable. It teaches you to control your breath and posture, two key components of mindfulness. Yet meditation also encourages you stop thought, which is a form of disengagement with the world. Meditation is valuable for relaxing and de-stressing. To become fully mindful, however, I prefer we take a more active approach.

My view of mindfulness is more active. I want to be fully immersed in experiences I find valuable. I want to rid my body of negative emotions, thoughts, and feelings while living my day-to-day life. How does that sound to you? Would you like to be more actively engaged in your life and live free of worry? How can you be physically active, mentally alert, and stay in the present moment?

It Takes Discipline to Become More Mindful:

Getting into the present moment is an active process involving discipline and self-awareness. In fact, you've already begun to develop these skills from the previous chapters. You now see why we covered self-talk and framing before discussing mindset. You realize already that self-talk, framing and focus will help you get into the present moment.

When you begin to notice your thoughts spiraling out of control (a lack of mindfulness), you use self-talk and framing techniques to bring your thoughts back under control.

Using Self-Talk and Framing Techniques to Become More Mindful:

Where are you, right now? Yes, I am talking to you through these pages.

Are you watching TV while skimming these words on the page? It's OK. I won't judge you. Don't judge yourself. Mindfulness, after all, is about perception rather than judgment. Use self-talk in the present moment right now. You might say, "I am sitting on the couch reading a book. I'm rushed and feel like I don't have enough time to finish it. The concepts are a bit esoteric. I don't know if this stuff will work for me. Where are the scientific studies?" In other words, right now you're judging the book, you're judging your experience.

Try this instead. "I am [insert where you are, what you are doing, what you are wearing, what you are sensing, in a non-judgmental way] reading a book to help me grow. I may not agree with everything in the book, but even not agreeing with someone can help me discover the truth. Disagreement allows me to examine my own core beliefs and values."

Do you see what we did there? You just checked in. You were conscious. You were engaged. You were mindful! Ultimately, that's your first step to developing mindfulness. Simply use self-talk to become aware of where you are and what you are doing. When you find yourself judging a person or an experience, reframe it. Instead of getting frustrated or angry by saying, "This is wrong," reframe the issue as, "This is a great opportunity for me to examine my own beliefs. I am improving by focusing on the opportunity for personal development and growth."

Mindfulness Is Learning to Control Your Inner Judge:

Our minds are constantly imposing meaning – sometimes false, often imagined - into perceptions. Our reality often comes from past experiences or even cultural brainwashing. To see this in action, read this sentence: "If you can raed tihs, you hvae a sgtrane mnid, too. Can you raed tihs? Olny 55 plepoe out of 100 can."

Most people can read that sentence, even though it's gibberish. In fact, many can read it quickly without any problem. When you keep the first and last letter of the word of words we are familiar with, our inner judge takes over and fills in the blanks. This heuristic is helpful. It helps us save time. Yet often this inner judge "fills in the blanks" with negative thoughts, feelings, and emotions, and thus, creates our perceptions about the world.

Mindfulness Is Checking In:

Many of you reading this have had this problem. You want to do something. Maybe it's talk to your boss about a raise or approach a girl you are attracted to. Your mind starts spinning out of control. Your breathing changes. You become "breathless," as your rapid breathing puts you in a mild state of hyperventilation. When your mind starts spinning out of control, you have lost your state of mindfulness. To regain your mindfulness, check into your thoughts and your body.

How to Check into the Present Moment:

The surest way to get into the moment is to become aware of yourself. Become aware of your body. The easiest way to become aware of yourself and your body, is to either start talking out loud or use self-talk to check into your environment.

It doesn't matter where you are. You can use mindfulness techniques anywhere. For example, I have a popular podcast on iTunes called *Mike Cernovich Podcast*. Before each episode, I use the very mindfulness techniques we're talking about to prepare myself for the show. Before speaking, I use self-talk (sometimes out loud, warm up my vocal cords) to check in. Here's an example: "I'm looking at a microphone. It's a silver orb with slots cut out that have a black sort of mesh under the slots. There is Blue written on it, the brand of the microphone. The B has a lightning bolt on it. There's a red light on the side of the microphone."

Rather than worry about the podcast topic, if I will make a mistake, or whatever else, I simply become engaged in the process of speaking. While checking in, I'm not trying to think brilliant thoughts. I merely become mindful and aware. Because of this, I have no anxiety when podcasting. In fact, I usually don't even use a script; instead I trust the process.

Go to Big Spaces to Become More Mindful:

Why do most great thinkers and philosophers talk about going to the mountains or into the wilderness? Why does the ocean calm people? Why are sunsets beautiful? We love mountains, oceans, and sunsets as they ease our anxiety by making us feel connected with something bigger than ourselves. It's much easier to be in the present moment when ocean waves are crashing.

How to Check into Your Body to Become More Mindful:

We often aren't even aware of our bodies unless we feel deep pain or great joy. Otherwise, we tend to not even realize that our bodies exist. Our brains are blobs residing in a meat sack. One powerful way to improve your mindfulness is to check into your body, to become fully aware of who you are. Find a way to become present in your body. You needn't be too creative here. Any small step helps.

> **GORILLA MINDSET SHIFT:** CHECK INTO YOUR BODY BY USING SELF-TALK TO UNDERSTAND WHAT YOUR BODY IS DOING AND FEELING IN THE PRESENT MOMENT.

Maybe you are sitting down on the couch reading this book. Are you lying flat on your back? Are you sitting up? Are you holding the book out in front of your face? Are you using an e-reader such as a Kindle? Your self-talk could go something like, "I'm lying on my back. I'm holding my Kindle out in front of me. I'm reading a book. My legs are stretched out over the edge of the couch. My neck is kinked slightly forward as I read."

Or maybe you're doing something entirely different. It doesn't matter! The Gorilla Mindset Shift to make is simply to become aware, to realize where you are and what you are doing without judgment.

PART 2: HOW TO USE MINDFULNESS TO ACHIEVE YOUR GOALS AND IMPROVE YOUR LIFE

We've looked at specific and practical things you can do to improve mindfulness. This will make you more alert, aware, and engaged with the present moment. It will lead to you feeling more positive and peaceful. But mindfulness goes beyond just affecting how you think and feel. These changes will also have a practical, physical impact in your life and your actions. Now that you understand the steps you can take to be more mindful, let's look at ways you can use that mindfulness to make real changes in the way you live your life.

Us Mindfulness to Improve Your Reading Comprehension and Focus:

Years ago, I began studying the work of Milton H. Erickson and his amazing book, *My Voice Will Go with You*. I used the same techniques and language patterns Erickson used to treat his patients during therapy when talking to myself. During my studies, I came across an amazing mindfulness exercise that improves reading comprehension. Although the exercise was not labeled as a mindfulness exercise, that's how I chose to frame it.

Since you're reading this book, you're obviously a voracious reader. Try this exercise from *Handbook of Hypnotic Suggestions and Metaphors* by D. Corydon Hammond before you begin reading, or when you otherwise want to improve your focus:

> *Notice the paper. What color is it? Notice how clean and crisp it seems. Fingers slide over the surface, and feel how smooth. Eyes can flow across the page, going easily from side to side, seeing everything. "Notice the letters on the page. They seem dark and distinct. The round parts of the O's and C's are very smooth; the up*

and down parts of the T's and L's are tall and strong. The printing is especially vivid. The words seem to stand out very clearly.

You've already become more mindful of the shapes of the very letters you're now reading. You are more present, aware, and actively engaged with what you are reading. You have "checked in" to *Gorilla Mindset* in a powerful way.

Indeed, you may find that this style of reading is difficult and mentally taxing at first. It is a challenge. Yet, as you become more mindful, your reading comprehension improves. By now you have learned to reframe "challenging" as an opportunity for growth.

How to Use Mindfulness to Move with Purpose:

One of my most popular podcasts was titled, "How to Move and Live with Purpose." That episode of the *Mike Cernovich Podcast* walked listeners through a mindfulness exercise I use when I walk. If you would like to listen to the podcast, you can find it for free at GorillaMindset.com/Podcasts

In the podcast, I noted my favorite activity is walking. Walking has been the pastime of the world's greatest thinkers. Aristotle, Plato, and Socrates were all famous for taking their students on walking lectures. Their philosophical discussions did not occur in the classroom. They would walk and talk.

Henry David Thoreau wrote an entire essay on how he would walk, think, and formulate ideas. I'm the same way. I walk all the time and I have my best ideas when I walk. I just get completely inside of my head and start moving. When your body moves, your mind and your brain move along with it, because everything is connected.

In the podcast, I explained how to use mindfulness to improve your posture while walking, and how improving your posture would change your physical gait, and even boost your mood.

Although it's most helpful to listen to the podcast while walking, the instructions are set forth below.

> **GORILLA MINDSET SHIFT:** WALK WITH A PURPOSE BY TALKING TO YOURSELF AS YOU WALK, ABOUT HOW YOU ARE WALKING.

To become one with your body, start paying attention to how you walk. Although we all know how to walk, many of us do so mindlessly. We have poor posture and our gait is lacking security and self-possession. Do you know how you walk? Most likely, you go heel-to-toe, heel-to-toe. Your pelvis is tight and your shoulders lean forward a bit. Our posture from sitting at work carries over to how we walk.

The next time you go for a walk, get in touch with your body. Start from your feet. Say to yourself, "My feet are striking the ground." Yes, actually use self-talk. You may say something like, "OK my feet are walking on the ground, touching the ground, left foot - right foot - left foot - right foot. Heel to toe, heel to toe."

While having this conversation, you will become aware of how your feet move when walking, which isn't something most of us are aware of. When walking, you tend to land on your heel. From there, you lean forward and propel yourself from the ball of your foot. That's not the way we have evolved to walk. We walk that way because we wear shoes. You want to start walking a bit differently and here's how you change that. Change the dialogue you have with your body.

Check into the present moment when walking. Use self-talk to say, "Heel to toe, heel to toe; I'm going to flex my calf a little bit." As you are walking just flex your calf a little bit on each step. You'll become aware of the balls of your feet, and your calves may even develop a slight "pump."

Continue with the conversation: "I feel the balls of my feet now. I feel how my foot flexes. I feel my arch. My calves are burning slightly." Even though walking is not rigorous, you're going to feel your respiratory and heart rate increase. Your pace will increase simply because you are flexing your calf.

The next step is to think about your gluteus muscles (your "glutes", or butt muscles). As you walk, start flexing your glutes with each step as your foot lands, and propel yourself with the ball of your foot. Your glutes will flex and it might will feel a little weird. Initially, you might not even know what you're feeling because a lot of people have what's called gluteal amnesia.

We have gluteal amnesia from sitting too much. We rarely use our glute muscles, as they are not activated while sitting. As you are walking and flexing your glutes, you start to realize that your legs might feel longer. And your hips might feel tighter, especially if you work in an office. This is due to anterior pelvic tilt. Anterior pelvic tilt occurs when your pelvis is tilting forward, rather than being properly aligned.

We deal with anterior pelvic tilt from sitting in chairs. When you sit down in a chair you lean forward slightly with your upper torso. This causes tightening in the hips. Walking helps to loosen up and reverse anterior pelvic tilt.

Do you see how everything is connected now? We started out with being mindful of how you walk. You may have thought, "I know how to walk!" But as you walk, you notice you're on the balls of your feet, then you begin flexing your glutes with each stride. Suddenly, your legs feel longer as your pelvis opens. Your hips are loosening up and you're moving forward.

When you walk this way, you feel more confident, more self assured. Why? You are not simply existing in your body. You are engaging with a sense of connectedness and purpose. Most people walk like mindless drones. That's because most are not aware of their bodies. They are "checked out."

Continue walking. You're on the balls of your feet, you're flexing your glutes, you're lengthening your hips. You are standing tall! Now pay attention to your chest. I bet you're like me and everybody else who works behind a keyboard. You're going to have what's called pronated shoulders. Pronated comes from the root *pro-*, which means forward. Your shoulders lean forward. Our pelvises tilt. We hunch forward. You are now aware of your body and realize the power of checking in.

Focus on your chest. Imagine that someone is grabbing you by the nape of your neck, much like a mama bear grabs the cub, and pulling you straight up. As your chest rises, you might notice a strain on your lower back. As you become one with your body, you realize how much effort it takes to stand with proper posture.

You're no longer treating your body like some abstraction. You are becoming aware of every muscle. You notice when you are walking that you have abdominal flexion, that is, your "core muscles" flexing. You'll start to feel your shoulders being drawn back. Suddenly your chin will rise. Look around you. Do you see most people have their chins hanging down?

Watch people walk. Their shoulders slouch and their chins are down from poor posture. They're not in touch with their bodies. Again, imagine somebody is pulling you straight up by the nape of your neck, your shoulders are drawn, your chin is up, and now you are walking the right way. Check in with your body. How do you feel? Present, powerful, and confident.

Practice walking. Notice how your gait changes. More importantly, notice how your mood improves. As you continue walking mindfully, you'll notice that your posture improves when standing. You'll have the posture of a soldier. You will stand and walk with pride, focus, and confidence.

How to Use Mindfulness to Deal with Anxiety:

Anxiety is caused by focusing on an uncertain event in the future. We humans tend to have the same anxieties, like money, friends, family, and health. We agonize over money, wondering how we will pay our bills. When you are worried about some uncertain future event, you're not living in the present moment. Active meditation and living mindfully doesn't mean that you ignore your problems. If you have money problems, then you should want to solve them.

Is being anxious going to solve that problem? Anxiety is an emotion that disempowers you and accomplishes nothing. When you learn how to get into the moment and engage in active meditation, you'll no longer feel anxiety. You'll have a sense of calmness going with the flow of life, rather than against it. *Flow* is a concept from a book called, *Finding Flow: The Psychology of Engagement with Everyday Life* by Mihaly Csikszentmihalyi.

As you practice your self-talk, you'll get into the moment and suddenly you won't feel anxious anymore. Why? The logical mind wants a logical explanation for why you stopped feeling anxious. Since anxiety is usually a feeling that comes from anticipating the future, anxiety is generally only about a possibility. You don't know what's going to happen tomorrow.

You don't know what's going to happen in the next minute, much less at a point further in the future, so why are you worrying about it? When you start living in the moment, you stop worrying about the future.

How to Use Mindfulness at the Gym:

I perform a mindfulness workout before lifting weights. I started this during my training sessions after watching a "day-in-the-life" video of professional bodybuilder, Kai Green. Kai Green is one of the world's top bodybuilders. He engages in brutal workouts.

Before each workout, he "checks in" using self-talk and mindfulness techniques. He asks himself why he is at the gym. He visualizes who he wants to become.

I used to find long warm-ups a bore and it took a lot of effort at first to complete them. I later realized boredom is the result of not being in the present moment. Here is an example of how to practice mindfulness at the gym:

1. Turn off your cell phone. (Even better, leave it in your car or gym locker.)
2. Get on a treadmill, exercise bike, or stair climber.
3. As your body starts moving, focus on having good posture.
4. Begin at a slow to moderate pace.
5. Ask yourself, "Why am I here? What do I expect to accomplish today?"
6. Begin to feel your blood circulating, your respiration increasing, and sweat forming.
7. Tell yourself that you are at the gym – working out to improve your body and mental clarity. Going to the gym is beneficial for your overall health, and you will feel much better afterwards.

You should also be mindful when lifting weights. There are people you see at the gym day after day, year after year, who never see any results. Partly because they are always talking with friends or looking at their cell phone.

Instead, check into your body. Feel each movement. You are at the gym to build your body. Stay focused.

How to Use Mindfulness to Create Deeper Connections:

To connect deeply with others, you must be present, mindful, and engaged.

Often, we talk to someone and feel like we're not being heard, like the person across from us is somewhere else.

To make deeper connections, you want the person you're talking with to feel like the only person in the room. Use mindfulness techniques to stay engaged.

When you feel distracted during a conversation, you can help yourself check in by using these two powerful mantras. I use them regularly, especially when there's a lull in conversation.

- There's no place else I'd rather be.
- There's no one else I'd rather see.

When you tell yourself this, you begin to believe it. When you believe that there is nowhere else you'd rather be and no one else you'd rather see, the other person can feel it.

You will make deeper, longer-lasting connections through this mindfulness technique.

As you can see, mindfulness is not something *woo-woo* or New Age.

Mindfulness is a mindset technique you can apply to all areas of your life.

THE MINDFULNESS WORKSHEET

When did you last feel "on," "in the zone," or in "the flow?"

You'll likely notice you have better workouts, or even days at work, when you warm up. A warm-up helps you get into the moment. Think back to a time you felt warmed up and prepared for action.

Write out what you did:

_____.

For example, I might write, "Before doing a podcast I started talking out loud. I talked about what was in the room. I took in deep breaths and exhaled deeply. This warmed up my vocal cords, helped prepare my voice for the podcast, and provided oxygen to my brain."

Check into Whatever Task You're about to Perform:

Before you begin a hard day at work, a workout, or even have a family dinner with the in-laws, check in. Ask yourself why you're doing what you're doing. Are you working hard to take care of your family?

Checking in will help you be more aware of your emotions and can make even the most challenging or mundane things more fulfilling.

    I am about to _____.

    I am going to do this because _____.

For example, I would write, "I am about to go to the gym. I going to the gym because I feel amazing afterwards. The hour or so of work in the gym makes the rest of my life feel amazing. I have more energy, vitality, and an overall sense of wellbeing."

If I were about to do something unpleasant, such as visit family who hold different beliefs, I may say, "I am going to visit my family. They are kind-hearted people who have always been there for me. Whatever annoyances I face are small in comparison to the largeness of their hearts."

Can you think of another way to become more mindful of life? If so, write it out and feel free to email it to me.

GORILLA MINDFULNESS HABITS

The detailed exercises we talked about will help improve your mindfulness and use it to improve your day-to-day life.

Do you want to push yourself even further, turning mindfulness into a practical part of your everyday life training? Here are some small changes you can make that will have big results:

- When you begin to feel an emotion, ask yourself, "Where do I feel this in my body?"
- Go big. Find an ocean, skyscrapers, waterfalls, mountains. Focus on the vastness of it. Imagine the waves crashing in.
- Buy an MP3 or CD with white noise or the sounds of rain falling.
- Buy a miniature waterfall.
- Listen to some house, trance, jazz, or classical music.
- Listen to deep vocal beats when writing. Rhythm, it's like running.
- When all else fails, practice self-talk. "Here I am, in the present moment."

10 Quick Ways to Become More Mindful:

Mindfulness is getting into the moment and becoming aware of yourself and your surroundings. Writers and artists are masters at noticing details others miss, as a writer must paint an image in the mind's eye of the reader.

Here are 10 ways to become more aware of your surroundings:

1. Notice the eye color of every person you interact with. Most people are either too busy looking at their computer screens, or they lack the self-confidence to make eye contact.

2. Pay attention to a person's features. How many wrinkles do they have? Do they have freckles or sun spots? Do you think they spend a lot of time in the sun?

3. Watch a person smile. Do their cheeks move or does the area around the eyes crinkle (the so-called "crow's feet").

4. Look at the person's shoulders. Do they slump? Do they protrude forward?

5. Look at a palm reading chart. Read your own palm. Is this arbitrary? Sure. There is nothing magical about reading your palm, but there is something magical about learning how to see details others don't see.

6. Sit in a coffee shop for an hour. Count the number of people who come in. Pay attention to their age, race, and gender. Try estimating how many customers the café has on a given day.

7. Pay attention to the size and shape of each word in this sentence. How many words does this paragraph contain?

8. Get out a stopwatch. Count the number of breaths you take in a minute. This will help you become more mindful of your breathing patterns.

9. Pick up your favorite book or check out your favorite website. Count the number of words in each sentence, the number of sentences in each paragraph, and the number of paragraphs on each page. Is there a pattern or cadence? If so, can you use that same pattern or cadence in your own writing?

10. Look around, wherever you are. Count the number of different colors you see.

There's nothing particularly special about those 10 habits. Make up your own if you want to. Mindful people notice what others don't. Once you notice details others miss, life becomes more interesting, as visionaries see where the patterns in all things.

CHAPTER 4

Mindset and Mood: How to Control Your State of Mind

Your state of mind is a concept much like your frame of mind. We've heard people talk about having the right "state of mind," but no one really explains what that means. What does it mean to talk about your "state" of mind?

What Is a State of Mind:

Your state is your mood, your emotions, or how you feel in the present moment.

The way we typically understand state of mind is a bit contradictory. On one hand, we are told even as children, "Learn to control your emotions!" But other than perhaps counting backwards from 10, we are never told how. Instead, state of mind is something we treat as being passive. It is simply a "given." We feel a certain way and we must accept that feeling.

When we feel good, we have a good day and treat people well. When we feel badly, we have a horrible day and treat people poorly. In some cases, people have horrible years or even miserable lifetimes, due to being controlled by their moods.

We've all heard the expression, "I woke up on the wrong side of the bed!" This is a recognition that "It's going to be one of those days," where nothing seems to go right. It is recognizing something about your state of mind. But it is also approaching it with an attitude of passiveness, of resignation. Thoreau referred to this as "quiet desperation." Why not take an active approach to our state of mind?

> **GORILLA MINDSET SHIFT:** I AM GOING TO TAKE AN ACTIVE APPROACH TO MANAGING MY STATE OF MIND.

How to Manage Your State of Mind:

The original exercises for managing your state of mind came from the groundbreaking book *NLP: The New Technology of Achievement*. Since then, others such as Tony Robbins have adopted and modified those exercises.

To change your state, you must first use the mindfulness exercises to check in. What is your default state? How do you feel generally? How do you feel right now, in the present moment?

For example, my default state is a bit stoic. I don't feel much at all. I accept life. While Stoicism is helpful when facing adversity, Stoics miss out on a major part of the human experience. The weakness of my state is that I often lack excitement and enthusiasm. I can also appear passive and uncaring to others. Sometimes my default "go with the flow" state makes me seem weak, when the truth is, I simply don't care about most of the stuff others find important.

Examples of default state:

- **Optimistic:** You are enthusiastic (some might say overly so) about life, like a puppy dog.
- **Negative:** You always see the downside of life and the worst in people. You constantly watch your back and call everything a scam.

- **In-between:** You feel moved by the good and the bad. You tend to accept whatever "life" gives you.
- **Resourceful:** You feel empowered to solve whatever problems come your way.

It doesn't matter what your default state is. Remember our mindfulness techniques. We are not judging our default state. We are accepting and understanding how we tend to generally feel.

4 Steps to Mastering Control Over Your State of Mind:

This exercise might seem a little "mystical" and touchy-feely. I felt weird after performing a variation of mental exercises that had been outlined in *NLP: The New Technology of Achievement*. The truth is, this stuff isn't that weird.

Your body and mind are connected. Your emotions are influenced both by your thinking and by how your body feels. Think of these exercises like an acting class. To get into a role, an actor must trick himself into believing he thinks, feels, and acts like someone else. The same principles actors have used for centuries apply here as well.

To perform these mental exercises, it's essential you are alone in a place where you feel comfortable to completely loosen up and "get weird." This is a private moment with yourself, not to do around other people. Mastering your mental state requires you to be honest with yourself, to dig deep, and be comfortable letting go. Unfortunately, most people never master a mental state as something inside them. Their inner judge or preconceived notions stop them from performing these exercises.

Here is how to master every mental state:

1. Go into a room by yourself.
2. Feel the emotions inside of your body.
3. Create your sphere of emotional space.
4. Reinforce your new mental state.

Step 1: To Find Yourself, Go at it Alone

Go somewhere you will not be distracted for at least 30 minutes. Do not bring anything into the room with you. Turn off the television, your smartphone, and any other distractions.

Remember when I said it's time to get weird? Now you'll see what I meant.

You are going to talk to yourself. (Remember, after the chapters on self-talk and mindfulness, talking to yourself isn't that weird!) The purpose of talking to yourself is to rewire your default state. Your default state (what we call "home base") is how you feel without trying to feel differently. It's how you "naturally" feel, without any additional effort.

When you're by yourself, begin saying: "I am resetting my home base, my default state is going to be one of empowerment, resourcefulness, and invincibility." You may want to feel an entirely different way. If so, that's fine and you can modify these exercises. What matters most is that you are taking control and deciding what your default state will be, instead of just treating your emotions or moods random occurrences.

Invincibility means you cannot be defeated unless you quit. Resourcefulness means believing you have the abilities and resources to solve any of life's problems. To change your default state, you must return to a time in your mind when you felt invincible, powerful, and resourceful.

Was there ever a time in your life when you felt on top of the world? Maybe you won the spelling bee as a kid, or had some success as an athlete. Or maybe you took the first step towards changing your life, which felt incredible. It doesn't matter how "big" or "small" your victory was, winning feels the same to your body, and we are capturing that feeling of victory. Avoid judging your achievements by trivializing them. Avoid saying, "This event where I felt invincible isn't big enough to care about."

You're not judging yourself because it's your life. If you felt great after asking someone out on a date, awesome! What matters is how you felt, not how others would have felt. Have you returned to a time in your life when you felt invincible? Fantastic.

Step 2. Feel Your Emotions Within

As you return to a moment of triumph, be mindful of what happens to your body. Become aware. Check in. How do you feel? Is your skin tingling? Do you feel a rush of blood throughout your body? Everyone will react differently to this mental exercise. For example, I feel blood and energy flow in my forearms. Others feel these exercises in their legs, shoulders, chest, or cheeks.

There is no wrong place to feel this energy. What matters is learning to feel this energy and become one with it. Pay attention to what is happening to both your body and your mind. As you monitor your body, you're also creating a new biofeedback loop between your emotional state and your physical state. You can return to a state of mental power by learning how to recreate these feelings of physical power. Since I feel energy in my forearms during this mental exercise, I will shake my forearms when I'm in a bad mood. Getting extra blood flowing to my arms improves my mood.

This may sound weird, but it really does work!

Instead of feeling like I'm losing confidence, I move my arms back and forth and I feel my state of resourcefulness returning to me. As you become more in touch with the connection between your body and mind, you too will be able to "trigger" emotions by moving your body.

Step 3. Create Your Sphere of Emotional Space

You now know how to "capture" feelings of power in your body. Before ending this exercise, close your eyes and start to breathe deeply. Imagine an orb of energy surrounding you. This is a "sphere of power." Imagine that this orb or force field is surrounding your body, protecting you from all the negative influences and emotions of the outside world.

I like to imagine having a cartoon bubble around me. This bubble is a metaphor for your "personal space." We all have a sense of personal space, which is generally about 18 inches away from our face. When a person invades our personal space, we feel threatened. What about our emotional space? Shouldn't it be equally important?

That's what the orb does! It's emotional space. When you create this orb of emotional space, even if you're surrounded by chaos, you'll feel powerful and safe.

Step 4. Reinforce Your New Mental State

Once you've gone into a room alone, dug deep into yourself and found that feeling of power in your body, you need to reinforce the new mental state.

Just like brushing your teeth or going to the gym, "mental exercise" is something you must do frequently. You cannot change your default state just by wanting to, or just by thinking about it, any more than you can become a star athlete by just thinking about sports. You must get your body into the habit of being in the state you want to be in. To form a habit, you need to practice consistently.

When starting off, it's helpful to perform the mental exercises several times a day. As your competency increases, you can reduce the exercises to a couple of times each week.

THE STATE OF MIND WORKSHEET

Think back to a time when you felt on top of the world. Write out this experience in as much detail as you can. If you are stuck, think about the "who, what, when, where, and why" of the situation. Write it out: _____.

Describe how you felt when you were on top of the world. Did you feel powerful, confident, resourceful, invincible, happy? There is no right or wrong answer here. This is about how you felt. Write it out, in as much detail as possible: _____.

As you imagine that feeling, describe what happens to your body. Do you feel increased blood flow to a certain part of your body? Do you perhaps stand or sit with a different posture? Did you lift your chin up? Write out what happens: _____.

How can you move your body to recapture the powerful emotion you felt? For example, I move my arms out away from my body. This triggers powerful feelings within myself. What do you do? Again, journal this feeling: _____.

Additional Notes:

Include anything else you need to add:

_____.

GORILLA MENTAL EXERCISE HABITS

Remember, How You Feel is Your Choice:

Remind yourself that you have the power to choose how you feel. Tell yourself, "How I feel is a choice I make in the present moment." Do not passively accept whatever emotional state happens to affect your body.

Capture and Recreate the Moment:

We all have good days and challenging days. When you are feeling especially good, resourceful, or confident, capture the moment. Track where in your body you have this feeling. Recreate this feeling when you're by yourself or having a "blah" day.

Find an Outlet:

Find a release valve for yourself. Sometimes it feels good to release the negative energy from your body. There's nothing wrong with shouting, just don't shout at your spouse, family, friends, or especially your children! For me, going to the gym is essential. When I must take time off due to work or an injury, my mood is harder to manage.

Continue Performing the Mental Exercises:

You will not master anything, let alone your emotions, after reading a few pages in a book. You must apply what you read and practice consistently.

CHAPTER 5

MINDSET AND FOCUS: HOW TO TAKE CONTROL OF YOUR ATTENTION

We live in an ADHD society where the demands on our time and consciousness are endless. Employers expect us to be on the clock 24/7. Spouses, family, and friends demand attention, too. We are also bombarded with advertisements, TSA threat levels, and negative messages from the evening or online news.

Our loss of focus can have disastrous consequences. Most work-related accidents are due to being distracted. CDC statistics show we are more likely to die at home than anywhere else. (Part of this is due to the amount of time we spend at home – the more often you do something, the more frequently good and bad outcomes occur - but a lack of attention plays a major role in accidents.)

Being Distracted Can Have Tragic Consequences:

John Smith (names have been changed to protect the family's privacy) was on his way to work. It was a day like any other day. He loaded up his car, hopped in, and began his morning commute.

He arrived at work, went into his office, talked to colleagues, and sat at his desk. After putting in a full day, he returned to his car and made a tragic discovery. He had forgotten his child in the car.

Rather than dropping his child off at daycare, he had left his baby in the car and the child died of dehydration. Unfortunately, this is not a hypothetical story. Children die each year after being left in the car by their loving, hard-working parents.

John Smith, like every other parent, had thousands of thoughts running through his mind. He was thinking about packing a lunch for his child, packing his own lunch, what vaccinations to get his child, and much more. Like most working parents, he was likely sleep deprived.

Focus on the essentials. Do not run on autopilot or become an automaton to routine. Check in. Failure to do so, sadly, could result in harm, or even death.

How to Regain Your Focus:

I knew a friend of mine had been planning a trip with another friend, and I wanted to hear how it went.

"How was your trip to Croatia, James?"

"We never went," he answered.

I couldn't believe it. "You were so excited about that trip!"

"We were, but Tony forget to renew his passport."

Now some may say Tony was irresponsible for not renewing his passport, but I would say he lacked focus.

Tony wasn't focused on what he absolutely 100% needed for his vacation. Like most of us, his mind was being pulled in a thousand directions. Which is another way of saying, he wasn't focusing on anything at all.

When planning a vacation, there are a lot of things to take care of, so it's easy to lose focus. Think about the last time you planned a vacation. All of this and more (especially if you're traveling with children) went through your head:

> *Did I put my vacation time in at work? Is now a good time to leave? What is going to happen to the project I'm working on? What am I going to wear? What will the weather be like? How many bags will I need to pack? Who will feed my cat? Did I pay my utility bill in advance? Do I have enough money saved? Can I really afford this? What happens if while I'm gone from work, my company realizes it doesn't need me anymore?*

While you certainly don't want your cat to starve, it's easy to find someone to feed your cat. You could still get on your flight even if you had to wait till the last minute to find someone to feed your cat. And while late fees are annoying, a late fee for a bill would be a small price to pay in the grand scheme of a major vacation. (These days, airlines have fees for everything, reframe a late fee or other oversight as a cost of your vacation.) If taking a vacation will cost you your job, then you were going to be fired soon anyway.

If you lost your ATM card or cell phone (both of which would present difficulties during your trip), you could still get from Point A to Point B. It'd be a hassle and it'd be frustrating, but you'd be OK.

However, you can't board without your passport!

Focus on what is essential. Of course, the non-essential details still matter, but treat them as what they are — non-essential.

For example, when I travel, I set my passport, wallet, and cell phone aside. The "holy trinity." I keep them in an area far away from the rest of my bags. I know that, no matter what, I need my passport, wallet, and cell phone.

If I left all my luggage or lost it, I'd still be OK.

Think about what you really need. What really matters to you? If you forget to do something, would your life really change for the worse?

You can use your newfound Gorilla Focus for life decisions, big or small. I never leave my apartment without checking for the "holy trinity."

When stepping outside of my door, before closing it, I stop. I feel for my wallet, cell phone, and keys. Because of this Gorilla Mindset habit, I have never locked myself out of my apartment.

Focus on the essentials.

How to Manage Distractions

If you've been paying attention, you now know that all of the Gorilla Mindset concepts work together.

When you feel distracted, engage in self-talk. Ask yourself: "What am I focusing on?" Return to the present moment. What do you need to accomplish? Check into what you need and check out of what you do not need.

Talk yourself through where you are and what you are doing. For example, right now I am on an airplane to Hanoi, Vietnam for a short vacation. I am writing this chapter on Gorilla Focus. I am also thinking about how to effectively market *Gorilla Mindset*. I opened a new window with a marketing idea. My mind has started spiraling out of control.

I return to the present moment by focusing on writing this chapter. My fingers connect with keys and words appear on the screen. Sentence-by-sentence, word-by-word, I continue writing. I will focus on selling the book once it's finished.

Change Your Focus:

We go from a state of distraction to hyper-focusing on trivial bullshit.

My WiFi won't work! Where is my food?! What's taking so long!?

Check in. You are focusing on negative energy. What you are focusing on is frustrating you, making you angry, and bringing you further away from feeling good about yourself and accomplishing your goals.

Tony Robbins says, "What you focus on is what you feel." If you focus on what is lacking (scarcity mindset) rather than what you have (abundance mindset), you will feel frenzied, frustrated, and angry.

Focus works both ways. You can focus on what matters or what doesn't. You can focus on what makes you feel rich and abundant, or what makes you feel inadequate and lacking.

Remember to check in. "Why am I focusing on trivial things?" Ask yourself, "Is focusing in this direction making me feel better or worse about myself or the situation I am in?"

Is your focus bringing you closer to feeling the way you want to feel or taking you further away?

Focus on Your Goals:

In *Pumping Iron*, a documentary about bodybuilding and Hollywood legend Arnold Schwarzenegger, we see the power of Gorilla Focus.

Arnold was focusing on his upcoming bodybuilding contest, Mr. Olympia. During the interview, Arnold was asked how he maintains his focus for the competition. How would he handle stress? Arnold told the interviewer, "*If someone steals my car outside right now, I don't care. I can't be bothered with that. All I can do is call the insurance agency and they'll laugh about it. I trained myself for that and not to let things go into my mind."*

Most of us would be angry if we went outside to see our car gone. What if we allowed our emotions to overtake us? That would add stress to our lives and be physically and emotionally draining.

Is it worth it? Is losing vital emotional, physical, and life-force energy worth it? Is losing our temper worth it?

Arnold refused to let any distraction get in the way of his goals and, as a result, he has lived the life other men dream of.

It's easy to become distracted and feel angry. You can overcome this is by checking in consistently, engaging in empowering and helpful self-talk, and returning your focus to what really matters.

Use self-talk to keep yourself accountable.

How to Use Self-Talk to Keep Yourself Focused and Accountable:

Ask yourself, in the present moment, "What am I focusing on?" If the answer is anything other than what really matters, ask yourself why.

Obviously, you can't focus on something non-stop. You are not a robot. Relaxation and leisure are necessary.

You had better have a good answer, though. "Because I want to be distracted," is not an acceptable answer. "Because I have Adult Hyperactivity Attention Disorder," is a cop out.

Not everyone has the luxury of going off the grid all day. But are you really so Mr. Important that you can't go off the grid for 30 minutes a day? I highly doubt it.

There's an interesting contradiction I've noticed among men. They claim that they can't put their cell phones down because they are just so damn important.

Have you ever considered your assumptions and the implications of them? If you were as important as you think, wouldn't people be dying for you to get back to them?

If Richard Branson wants to go off the grid, can he? Do you think Steve Jobs scrambled to answer his emails?

You're Not Warren Buffett:

Warren Buffett is the second richest man in the world. He goes to his office from 8 a.m. to 6 p.m. and he doesn't answer email.

In fact, you can't claim to be free if you're accessible 24/7. The more plugged in you are, the less importantance you're placing on yourself.

Being plugged in and connected does not signal importance. It shows that you are a slave to others.

Take charge. Disconnect. Focus.

How to Develop Gorilla Focus:

Our focus is our attention, which we well understand. What is it about our focus that should be ruthless? Our focus is ruthless because we must cut out all people and activities distracting us from what we want.

Ask these questions to develop ruthless focus:

1. What do you want more of?
2. What do you want less of?
3. Does [person/activity] bring you more of what you want?

4. Does [person/activity] bring you less of what you want?

We are the sum of our activities and the people we surround ourselves with. Yet we often give people a "friends and family pass" when they engage in nonsense. Because of this, our friends and family are really "friends" and "family" who see us as people to exploit.

But your life belongs to you, not them. If people want to associate with you, it must be on your terms. Those who do not want to meet your terms are free to leave. The same is true of other people. If you live a self-indulgent life where you always seek to use others for your own benefit, don't cry when you find yourself alone.

Goals are positive outcomes you desire in your life.

For example, you don't set a goal to die in a car crash. You set a goal because you believe achieving that goal (or the process of achieving it) will have a positive outcome on your life. What positive outcome do you desire?

Positive outcomes include happiness, financial freedom, free time, a healthier body, better relationships, more travel, and whatever else you desire. It's important to determine the positive outcomes you desire. Otherwise, it's simply not possible to develop focus, let alone ruthless focus.

In a way, I'm the man who has everything, even though I don't have a private jet, a yacht, or 5 girls in my bed. (If I wanted those things, I'd change my focus to help me obtain them.)

However, there are some things I want less of. We call what we want less of "negative outcomes."

Negative outcomes include depression, stress, hatred, anger, sickness, disease, jealousy, outrage, negativity, annoyance, anxiety and whatever you want less of.

What do you want less of? If you want to feel less angry, why do you read news sites or watch TV? Television and media primarily exist to instill fear, shock, and outrage within you. Should you be focusing your attention on negative outcomes?

Asking these four ruthless-focus questions will help you decide whether what you're about to do fits in with your desired outcomes.

For example, I do not want more stress in my life. To make more money, you often must endure more stress. If I wanted more money, I might deal with more stress to make more money. Yet this decision to accept the stress would be mindful rather than thoughtless. I would be able to cope with the stress, recognizing that it was bringing me closer to a positive outcome. I would be making a conscious choice.

When someone offers me a deal, I use ruthless focus and ask myself, "Are you doing this only for the money? If so, then you cannot say yes." Money is tempting, but I've learned that a business deal that involves money without passion doesn't excite me. Money isn't enough. A new venture must make a difference in the lives of others.

Conduct an inventory of everyone and everything in your life. Ask yourself: Does [insert the person] increase your [insert positive outcome]? Does [insert the activity] increase your [insert positive outcome]?

It may seem cruel or, indeed, ruthless, but that is what it takes to succeed.

Focusing on What You Want in Life Is Not Selfish:

As you develop more focus in your life, you may notice people calling you selfish. People who accuse you of being selfish are twice as selfish as they claim you are.

I'm a pretty low-key guy. I rarely ask anyone for anything. Usually it's people trying to get at me to sell me something, to guilt me into helping them, or con me into giving them something. When I say no, they act like it's immoral on my part. "Mike is so selfish!" By saying no, I am not compelling anyone to do anything. I am not imposing my will on anyone. I am simply asking to be left alone.

When people insist that you do what they want, they are attempting to control your life. They are the ones being selfish.

When you develop ruthless focus, you may learn that many of your friends and family members aren't friends at all. They are people who use you for their own ends and become deeply offended when you start living your own life.

Do you want those people to remain in your life? If so, why? They will bring you more negative outcomes than positive. There is no reason to continue unhealthy relationships, be it intimate, family or friend. On the plus side, those who are winners will recognize and appreciate your ruthless focus.

True friends want to see you succeed. They want what is best for you.

If your friends and family can't "chill" while you do you for a while, good riddance.

Developing ruthless focus will leave you with a stronger circle of friends while ridding your life of the dead weight. Answer these questions to develop ruthless focus:

1. What do you want more of?
2. What do you want less of?
3. Does [person/activity] bring you **more** of what you want?
4. Does [person/activity] bring you **less** of what you want?

YOUR GORILLA FOCUS WORKSHEET

What is one thing in your life you want more of? This could be anything, including more money, more love, better relationships, or even bigger muscles. It's not my place to judge you. If you can, include a reason for why you want more of something.

Write it out: _____.

For example, "I want more money because having more money will give me the freedom to pursue my dreams."

What is one thing you want less of in your life? This could be less stress or it could even mean fewer friends. Some of us have too many people demanding our time and attention and thinning out our Rolodex might be a wise move. As with the exercise above, include a reason why you want less of that one thing.

Write it out: _____.

For example, "I want fewer social obligations because hanging out with other people drains me." Now, ask yourself this question: Are you focusing on ways to get more of what you want and less of what you don't want?

Write out how you are (or are not) focusing on what matters most in your life: _____
_____.

To regain our focus, we must first determine what it is we intend to focus on. While this is a personal choice affected by your lifestyle, most of us want better relationships, more money, and improved health and fitness.

GORILLA FOCUS HABITS

Recognize That Focus is Either/Or:

Countless studies have proven humans are not capable of multi-tasking. At best, we can switch from one task to another effectively, but we lose our flow when we do.

When you feel yourself focusing on something, ask yourself if you are focusing on what matters.

Use Self-Talk to Recognize What You're Focusing On:

Ask yourself, "What am I focusing on? Why am I focusing on this? Is focusing on this issue/person/idea bringing me closer to my goals or pushing me further away?" As you see, focus is tied to your self-talk and mindfulness. The more checked in you are, the more focus you have.

Focus Is Finite:

Our human willpower and ability to focus is limited. (That topic is covered in the next chapter.) Avoid depleting your ability to focus by wasting it on negativity or toxic people. Organize your life to maximize your focus.

Focus on Good Health:

Focus requires brain power, which requires peak physical health. To increase your focus, follow the health and fitness guidelines in Chapter 7.

Focus on What Matters Most in Your Life:

By taking inventory of your life, you'll begin to understand who and what you want in it. Focus on obtaining more of what you want out of life while refusing to focus on negative people and activities.

Use Self-Talk to Regain Your Focus:

When you feel your mind wandering, use self-talk to remind yourself, "I am choosing to focus on x, when I should be focusing on y."

Turn Off Your Cell Phone at The Gym:

When I am at the gym I turn off my cell phone. The gym is time away from the grind, and it's a time to focus on my health and fitness.

Turn Off Your Cell Phone When Playing with Your Children:

They are the most important people in your life. Mindlessly checking email and being distracted is something they will notice and remember. Turn the phone off.

Do Not Eat in Front of the Television:

When you eat, you should focus on your food. Studies have shown people tend to eat 25-50% more calories when eating in front of the television. Because we aren't focused on eating while watching television (or surfing the web), we lose track of how much we've actually eaten.

Pick One Task to Accomplish at a Time:

The world is busy and we're overwhelmed, but you work most effectively when you focus on one task at a time. Choose one task and work on that for a set period of time. (I work in 45-minute intervals, and take 5-15 minutes to goof off and decompress).

CHAPTER 6

MINDSET AND LIFESTYLE: CHANGE THE WAY YOU LIVE

You now understand the power of mindset. You have the habits and skills you need to change the way you think, look, and feel. These new mindset shifts will improve your health and fitness, personal finances, and relationships. Yet we often make it harder to apply the Gorilla Mindset principles to our lives than it should be.

> **GORILLA MINDSET SHIFT:** YOUR LIFESTYLE AND MINDSET ARE LINKED.

What Is a Lifestyle:

Psychologist Alfred Adler observed, that lifestyle is, "the interests, opinions, behaviors, and behavioral orientations of an individual, group, or culture." Lifestyle is how you live your life– what you eat, drink, where you live, the people you spend your time with, and the activities you engage in.

Is it easier or harder to control your mental state and mood after you've had a full night's sleep? Are you more, or less able, to check into the present moment when your smartphone isn't buzzing at you? Are you more likely to feel an "attitude of gratitude" when you're around warm, kind, and generous people?

We often view mindset defensively. We use our mindset techniques to overcome obstacles and turn problems into a source of power. Imagine how much more powerful these techniques will be when you start using them offensively – when you use these techniques to take your life to the next level, rather than to merely get you out of a rut.

If the only message you took away from *Gorilla Mindset* were to cut out toxic people from your life, then I'd consider this book a massive success.

> **GORILLA MINDSET SHIFT:** AVOID NEGATIVE SITUATIONS AND DRAINING PEOPLE, INSTEAD CHOOSE TO ENGAGE IN LIFE-AFFIRMING ACTIVITIES WITH POSITIVE, HELPFUL PEOPLE.

Cut Off Contact with Negative People, Even Family Members

The more people you have in your life, the more fulfillment or stress. When you allow negative people in your life, you begin using the Gorilla Mindset techniques defensively. You are fighting off stress and anxiety rather than pushing forward toward your goal.

Say No to Everything:

Chances are, you are already too busy. You need time to work on yourself. You don't have time to allow others to impose their demands and ego upon you. For the next four weeks, say no to everything someone asks you to do. If you do insist on saying yes to some requests, heed this rule: "Never make a promise when you're in a good mood." We are more likely to overcommit ourselves when in a good mood.

Sleep as Much as You Can:

Sleep as much as you need to. Yes, life is busy and we all have reasons to lose sleep. I'm not going to lecture you on the need for enough sleep, as that's a choice only you can make.

GORILLA MINDSET SHIFT: THERE IS NOTHING COOL ABOUT "POWERING THROUGH" SLEEP DEPRIVATION

Get white noise or anything that helps you sleep. I run a fan. Sleeping with a humidifier next to the bed, especially when its dry out, is also a source of white noise and moisturizes your skin. Buy the best mattress and bedding you can afford. You spend one-third of your life in bed. I have found a foam memory topper (such as a Tempurpedic) is a game changer. Reflect on what you seek to achieve the next day. Too many people dwell on what happened during the day. Keep looking forward. Focus on your goals and life vision.

Health and Fitness:

While it'd be impossible to give a total dietary makeover here, there are some good guidelines to follow in the next chapter. Be exposed to fresh air and open spaces every day. Never sit for longer than one hour. Numerous scientific studies have shown that sitting is deadly. People who spend more hours a day sitting die sooner than those who stand up more often. Also, once you sit longer than one hour, fat loss shuts down for your body. Stand up, stretch, or go for a walk. I stand up every 30 minutes or so. When you remain hydrated, you'll naturally get up frequently. Stay hydrated. My goal is 8 trips to the bathroom a day, and to wake up with clear urine.

Perform the abundance posture poses, which are discussed in Chapter 8. You can do the posture excises sitting or standing.

Turn off electronic devices for as long as you can afford to. I do not use my smartphone at all when driving or when at the gym. (If I need to listen to music, I put my smartphone in airplane mode.) For at least two hours each day I am totally disconnected. This has done much for my levels of inner peace and mindfulness.

Do something physical each day. You don't have to hit the gym at full intensity. Sometimes "something physical" is simply taking a leisurely walk, or even getting a massage.

Establish a Morning Routine:

Some have said breakfast is the most important meal of the day, a recognition that your day begins in the morning. Although it seems obvious to point out that your day begins with your morning, how many of you have a morning routine that sets you up for a successful day?

The usual morning routine goes a little like this: Alarm goes off, wake up, hit snooze button, hit snooze button, hit snooze button, lay in bed, check an email or Internet news, rub your eyes, make some coffee, do your daily hygiene/shower. Most of us are defeated before we even get out of bed. We stay up too late and wake up exhausted. We press the snooze button several times. Our mindset is in a negative place.

"Another day, another dollar," is too often how we view our working lives. One day is the same as the next. As Henry David Thoreau wrote, "The mass of men lead lives of quiet desperation. What is called resignation is confirmed desperation."

GORILLA MINDSET SHIFT: YOU ARE AN ELITE ATHLETE IN THE GAME OF LIFE WHO MUST PROPERLY WARM UP FOR AN INTENSE AND INSPIRATIONAL COMPETITION.

The momentum of your day begins with your morning routine. Your perfect morning will lead to your perfect day, which will lead to a better life. End this life of quiet desperation by beginning your day with an empowering morning routine. Never press the snooze button. We know you're tired. Everyone is tired first thing in the morning. If you feel like you're about to fall asleep, get right out of bed. Rush into the shower. Take a contrast or cold shower. Perform a mindset-shifting brain exercise.

> **GORILLA MINDSET SHIFT:** A COLD OR CONTRAST SHOWER IS AN EMPOWERING WAY TO START THE DAY.

Benefits of a Cold Shower:

Cold showers have been around for centuries, with Spartan warriors taking a cold shower each day to jolt them into reality. Cold showers have made a resurgence with the writing of Victor Pride, who writes a website called *Bold & Determined* and advises people to take cold showers in his book *30 Days of Discipline*.

A cold shower can raise testosterone levels, lower cortisol levels, boost your immune system, and increase your mental toughness. Cold showers also work as a form of cardio, as you'll quickly find your heart pumping to warm your limbs. Cold showers have even been used to treat mild symptoms of depression, and some hypothesize cold showers may be beneficial in the treatment of Chronic Fatigue Syndrome.

At the very least, a cold shower will wake you up. Another side benefit of cold showers is cold water does not dry your skin. Your skin will be softer and more hydrated after getting out of a cold shower.

Cold showers take some getting used to. Rather than rushing right in, it's often helpful to ease into cold showers. Start off by running cold water on your arms and legs. Only then submerge your head and chest under the cold water.

Benefits of a Contrast Shower:

Having taken cold showers and contrast showers, I've learned contrast showers work more effectively for me. Contrast showers have been shown to help you recover from hard workouts, as they increase the circulation of lymphatic fluid and improve blood flow. Contrast showers also improve blood circulation and reduce feelings of stress.

When taking a contrast shower, start off by running warm to hot water. Run the hot water over your body for 30-60 seconds. Then switch the water all the way to cold. For 30-60 seconds, remain under the cold water.

Switch back between hot and cold water 3-5 times, finishing with the water set to cold. While you're in the shower, perform the Gorilla Mindset brain warm-up discussed in the next section.

The Gorilla Mindset brain warm-up is adopted from *The Complete Mental Fitness Book: Exercises to Improve Your Brain Power* by Tom Wujec.

Perform this five-minute brain warm-up each morning before getting out of bed:

1. Count backwards from 100. Speed is key. Don't stop if you skip a number. You are not trying to get everything 100% accurate, and given you may have just woken up, it's likely you'll skip a number.
2. Find a noun that fits each letter of the alphabet. A noun is a person, place, thing, or idea. Don't just think of an object. Imagine the colors and shapes and sizes of the noun. This will

activate your right brain (colors, images, shapes, sizes) and left brain (verbal, think of a word) simultaneously. This "brain crosstalk" will improve your overall cognitive performance.

For example:

   a — apple

   b — boy

   c — crabapples

   d — etc.

3. Create a numbered list of female names, 1-10. Say the number and letter to yourself or out loud. For example:

   1 — Lisa

   2 — Tina

   3 — Sherry

   4 — etc.

4. Create a numbered list of male names, 1-10. As with the female names above, say the number and letter to yourself or out loud. For example:

   1 — Edward

   2 — Tom

   3 — Bob

   4 — etc.

5. Close your eyes and take 10 deep meditative breaths. As you breathe deeply, focus on oxygenating your brain. You should feel the blood vessels and capillaries surrounding your brain start to expand. Then open your eyes.

You are now prepared to start your day. Does that seem like a lot of work? Perhaps. Although it may seem like a lot of work, it only takes 5-15 minutes to perform.

> **GORILLA MINDSET SHIFT:** "MY DAY IS A SERIOUS ATHLETIC ENDEAVOR THAT REQUIRES ME TO ACTIVELY WARM UP MY BODY AND MIND."

Some days you will think to yourself, "I don't feel like doing a warm-up." But ask yourself, "Would I warm up before lifting weights or playing a game of basketball?" Even golfers stretch before playing a leisurely 9 holes. Life is far more taxing than playing golf. Why would you warm up for a game of golf but not warm up for the serious game of life?

How to Improve Your Willpower:

*This chapter includes a bonus interview with Dr. Jeremy Nicholson

Willpower has always been a fascinating subject. We tend to believe our failures in life are due to a lack of willpower. But what exactly is willpower? And how can we get more and make the most of it? I was able to sit down with Dr. Jeremy Nicholson — a Social and Personality Psychologist— to discuss the limits of willpower. Here is the interview:

Mike Cernovich: What is willpower?

Dr. Nicholson: As opposed to animals (like lizards) that primarily live in the moment, we have an added component to our consciousness called Symbolic Self Awareness (Sedikides & Skowronski, 1997). That added awareness allows us to imagine future behaviors and their possible outcomes (like buying snacks at the store), before we actually act them out in real life (and pig out at home).

Essentially, it makes such future projections, plans, and goal-setting possible on a cognitive level.

As a result of this added symbolic awareness, we have the ability to improve ourselves by bouncing back and forth between setting future goals and immersing ourselves in present actions to reach those goals. This behavior has been described as a discrepancy-reducing feedback loop, also known as a test-operate-test-exit loop (Carver & Scheier, 1982). In essence, we project into an imagined future to set goals and plan (the test). We then perform behaviors in the present to get closer to those desired goals (operate). After a period of time, we compare the present to the future, in order to monitor our progress toward that future goal again (test). Finally, we either adjust and behave again (operate), or reach our set goal (exit).

This is the basics for why we flip-flop between present and future, in order to help us set and reach desired goals, and improve ourselves. It is also what Mike basically does to set plans and then "coast" through his day. HOW he (and we) accomplish these activities is a bit more complicated.

Mike Cernovich: How can we increase our willpower?

Dr. Nicholson: To begin, an individual needs to project into the future and set a goal. Such goal-setting is essential because goals are the "test" that all present action will be measured against. In Mike's world, it is the time he spends envisioning his ideal physique and deciding on the general steps and goals required to get there. Those goals, in turn, help to direct attention to goal-relevant activities, increase motivation, prolong effort, and aid in strategizing for future success (Locke & Latham, 2002). To best accomplish that, goals should:

- Be Specific — so that an individual can clearly measure success (e.g. deciding to lose 20 pounds is better than just wanting to lose weight).

- Be Challenging — in order to improve motivation and satisfaction upon completion. However, it should also be achievable, to avoid discouragement (e.g. setting a 20-pund goal instead of 5, because it is still achievable, but would make a bigger difference).
- Be Important — to meeting the person's needs (e.g. losing weight to promote health AND attractiveness).
- Provide Feedback — to help the individual be aware when change in behavior is needed (e.g. weighing every week to determine weight loss — or getting a DEXA scan every few months).

Next, it is important to motivate the behaviors required to reach the goal. We "perform" in the moment by being propelled by two general types of motivation (Ryan & Deci, 2000). We may perform because of personal desires, needs, or values internal to ourselves (Intrinsic Motivation). We may also take action to obtain some sort of external reward, favor, or relationship (Extrinsic Motivation).

Although both types of motivation serve the same function, when possible, it is often better to set goals and perform behaviors that are at least congruent with intrinsic motivations and personal needs. That is why people who work "doing what they love" are often more satisfied and productive than those who work "for a paycheck". It is also why Mike says that he doesn't fight himself, and is true to who he is and what he wants. He is being congruent with his intrinsic motivations and using them to drive his behavior.

To stay on track, self-control is important. Staying in the moment, keeping focused, and persisting is not always easy. That is where discipline and self-control come into play. However, self-control tends to operate like a muscle, getting fatigued with repeated use (Muraven & Baumeister, 2000). Therefore, try to juggle too many tasks in a day and you're bound to let one slip. Fortunately, also like a muscle, self-control gets stronger after repeated exertion and rest.

Thus, to perform in the moment and reach goals, self-control needs to be used judiciously. Ideally, goals and behaviors should be staggered, to give time for rest and recovery. New endeavors should be added one at a time. If that is not possible, then sometimes certain taxing behaviors or routines could be made more automatic and effortless with practice (Bargh & Chartrand, 1999). At other times, perhaps a change in general mood or reframing the task might make it less taxing — called Emotion-Focused Coping (Lazarus & Folkman, 1984).

This is the area where Mike really shines. He streamlines many of his tasks to make them automatic. He keeps a positive focus, reducing stress and making things feel less like "work." In short, he makes careful use of his limited self-control to maximize success.

Finally, it is important to "test" again and adjust behaviors as necessary to reach goals. That is where the idea of Implementation Intentions comes into play (Gollwitzer, 1999). In short, Implementation Intentions are quick "If X, then Y" statements, that lead to behavior prompts much like conditioned reflexes, or NLP anchors.

For example, if Mike sets certain times to fast, looking at the clock will automatically remind him about his diet (and not to eat yet). Similarly, if he associates certain dominant behaviors with the gym environment, those stimuli will prompt him to "hit it hard" when he walks in. Like Mike, by setting and conditioning these prompts, we can create little behavioral reminders that either keep us on track or help us change focus.

Overall then, looking into the future to plan and acting in the moment are two sides to the same coin of self-development. Switching between those states helps us to set goals, find motivation, control ourselves, and implement positive behaviors. Like with Mike, a little forethought also helps to reduce the clutter in our lives, reduce stress, and find greater success.

Now that you've read my thorough analysis of the mechanisms behind Mike's success … take one more cue from him. Spend a few minutes setting a goal, then get off your computer and go do it!

About Dr. Jeremy Nicholson:

Jeremy Nicholson is a Social and Personality Psychologist, whose research and writing focus on influence, persuasion, dating, and relationships. He also holds a master's degree in Industrial/Organizational Psychology and Social Work. Dr. Nicholson shares his advice as a dating/relationship expert as *The Attraction Doctor* on Psychology Today.

THE LIFESTYLE WORKSHEET

Organizing your lifestyle to optimize your mindset development and personal growth is an ongoing process of trial and error. Do not be afraid to experiment and tweak your lifestyle regularly. You want to improve the people you surround yourself with, the foods you eat, the type of exercise you engage in, and even the amount of time you spend on your smartphone.

How can you arrange your life to develop the right mindset? To answer that question, think about what your lifestyle is. Your lifestyle is the sum total of how you spend your time, and that means what you spend your time on and who you spend your time with. Who — and what — creates positive energy in your life? Who sucks away your energy like a vampire?

Who creates negative energy or drama in your life? Is it possible to disengage from them?

I will avoid _____, _____, and _____ because those situations drain me.

I will seek out _____, _____,
and _____ because, while those situations are stressful, they lead me to personal growth and enlightenment.

As with the other sections, this worksheet is far from comprehensive. Only you know your life. This worksheet is merely a starting point to help you reflect more upon the lifestyle choices you make, and how those choices impact your state of mind.

LIFESTYLE HABITS THAT WILL CHANGE YOUR MINDSET

Keypoints to Remember:

- Your lifestyle is the sum total of how you spend your time. This includes the activities you engage in and the people you associate with, whether at work, home, or online. To improve your lifestyle, improve the quality of people you socialize with as well as the activities you participate in.
- Take a cold shower or a contrast shower each morning.
- You want to be alert and prepared to start your day off right. A cold shower or contrast shower will wake you up, get blood flowing, and boost your immune system. Start your day off from a position of alertness.
- Perform the brain warm-up discussed in the previous section.
- Remember, you are an athlete participating in the challenging game of life. You must be prepared for anything and everything life may bring to you.
- Eliminate negative people from your life by following the Ruthless Focus exercise.
- The "Ruthless Focus" exercise could have been placed in lifestyle, as your lifestyle will be influenced by your focus. If

you focus on negative activities and people, your lifestyle will suffer. If you focus on positive activities and inspiring people, your lifestyle will soar.

- Before bed, reflect on your day.
- When reflecting on what you achieved (or not) during the day, do not be judgmental. Be mindful. Reflect on how you can improve tomorrow.

CHAPTER 7

MINDSET AND THE BODY: HEALTH AND FITNESS

While it would be impossible to discuss everything about your physical health here, there are some pillars of health that are important to understand. These are concepts you may not be familiar with, even if you are advanced in your knowledge of health and nutrition. Too many books on health and fitness are vague or theoretical, and don't focus on what will work for you as an individual.

What I'd like to do is introduce you to some concepts you can apply to your life. Experiment with yourself. Learn about your own body and the mind-body connection. Our focus will be on specific, practical things you can focus on and apply to become more in touch with your physical body, and understand what works for you, both physically and mentally.

Every day I keep these principles in mind. I try to do something to maintain or improve my blood, breath, posture, lymph, and digestion.

Blood Flow and Mindset:

You can't make the most of your mind if you don't have blood pumping to your brain. Research has shown the best way to improve your mind is to improve your heart. Ralph Sacco, M.D. and former president of the American Heart Association observed, "Most people don't understand the connection between heart health and brain health, and as doctors we're learning more every day."

Dr. Sacco advises patients who want to maintain a healthy mind throughout life to focus on improving their heart health, observing, "New studies have shown that the risk factors that can lead to heart disease and stroke, such as physical inactivity and obesity, also contribute to dementia, Alzheimer's disease, memory loss and cognitive dysfunction."

GORILLA MINDSET SHIFT: THE HEART AND MIND ARE CONNECTED. IF SOMETHING IS GOOD FOR YOUR HEART, IT'S GOOD FOR YOUR MIND.

The human heart pumps out approximately two thousand gallons of blood each day — enough to fill a home swimming pool. The heart pumps nutrient-rich blood to each of your trillions of cells every minute. Therefore, you want efficient blood flow throughout your body. You want your heart working at peak performance, and your vascular system pumping your blood efficiently. You also want your blood to contain the nutrients your body needs for growth and repair.

The scientific term for "good blood flow" is "endothelial function." Endothelial function refers to the ability of arteries to dilate properly. Dilated arteries are open, allowing blood to flow freely. A heart attack is caused by a blood clot. When you have endothelial dysfunction, you're at a greater risk for a heart attack. Your body is also less efficient and you're less intelligent, as blood does not pump throughout the body and to your brain.

How to Improve Endothelial Function:

A study published in *Physiological Reports* in January of 2015 has confirmed what many people have known and said for a long time: endothelial function can be improved by weight control with exercise and a healthy diet. Fruits and vegetables, especially those rich in flavonoids, improve endothelial function. Nitrate-containing foods like beets and beet juice also improve endothelial function.

Flavonoid-rich foods include:

- Blueberries
- Raspberries
- Blackberries
- Lemons
- Limes
- Oranges
- Grapefruit
- Apples
- Grapes
- Peppers
- Onions
- Broccoli
- Fresh herbs

To improve your body's ability to move blood and nutrients throughout your body, exercise daily. There are also supplements you can take to improve endothelial function.

Supplements and Food That Improve Blood Flow:

If an activity or supplement boosts blood flow, it's good for you. (Caution: Some people are on medications that may be contraindicated. Always consult with your doctor before starting a supplement.)

My grandfather had a heart attack at 65. When he went into the doctor's office, he was told that my grandmother saved his life. My grandmother had made my grandfather take an aspirin each day. The "aspirin a day keeps the heart attack away" is not an old wives' tale. The Mayo Clinic describes the process: "Aspirin interferes with your blood's clotting action. If your blood vessels are already narrowed from atherosclerosis — the buildup of fatty deposits in your arteries — a fatty deposit in your vessel lining can burst. Then, a blood clot can quickly form and block the artery. This prevents blood flow to the heart and causes a heart attack. Aspirin therapy reduces the clumping action of platelets — possibly preventing a heart attack."

Aspirin is a cheap way to improve blood flow throughout the body. Experts generally recommend 81 milligrams (a "baby aspirin") each day.

Beet juice and l-arginine (an over the counter supplement) also improve endothelial function by increasing the amount of nitric oxide in your body. Nitric oxide (NO) allows your blood vessels to dilate. Several studies have been dedicated to the relationship between nitric oxide and blood flow, and all of them show a positive relationship between NO, good blood flow, and overall health.

Breath and Mindset:

We all know that aerobic and anaerobic exercises are good for us, but how does that relate to mindset? Learning to control your breathing will improve your mindset. When feeling stressed or anxious, you've no doubt noticed a change in your breathing patterns. When you feel overwhelmed, your breath increases and stress can make your breathing shallow. You hyperventilate.

> **GORILLA MINDSET SHIFT:** TO MASTER YOUR MINDSET, MASTER YOUR BREATH.

Hop on the exercise bike or treadmill. I prefer the exercise bike, as I don't want to risk losing my balance, but a treadmill works fine. Move your body until your heart rate is in the 150-170 beats-per-minute range. Your heart should be pumping at a fast rate and you should become short of breath, which means you won't be able to comfortably carry on a conversation. As you feel your breath rate increase, pause. Take a deep breath. Hold it. Release it. Focus on controlling your rate of breathing, rather than letting your body arbitrarily dictate your breathing. While this will be challenging, it will help you take control of your breath during stressful times in your life. (Caution: Do not pass out or take this exercise too far, and always consult a doctor before undergoing any exercise program.)

Posture and Mindset:

Posture keeps your organs aligned, your balance proper, and decreases your risk of falling and thus, injury. It also makes you appear taller, more confident and physically attractive. Good posture can boost your mood, increase your testosterone levels, and even improve your breathing.

> **GORILLA MINDSET SHIFT:** STRONG POSTURE, STRONG MIND.

For that reason, there is an entire chapter on posture.

Lymph and Mindset:

The lymphatic system carries a clear fluid called lymph through the body. Your lymphatic system keeps your immune system healthy by transporting white blood cells (which fight off infections) and other immune-boosting cells throughout your body.

> **GORILLA MINDSET SHIFT:** A SICK BODY LEADS TO A SICK MIND.

Lymph fluid circulates throughout the body, and is used to recycle tissue fluids back into the bloodstream. It is critical to fighting off disease and toxins, as well as transporting healthy materials, like enzymes and hormones, throughout the body.

How to Improve Your Lymphatic System Function:

Lymph is moved throughout the body via physical movement. When you stretch, walk, or flex your muscles, lymphatic fluid is pumped towards your heart. (If you haven't figured it out already, being active every day is essential for all areas of your mental and physical health.)

Exercise is the best way to boost your lymphatic flow, but there are some other ways too. Wear compression garments. Compression garments, like tights or even Underarmor, press lymphatic fluid up towards your heart.

Taking a contrast shower also boosts lymphatic flow. Warm or hot water causes blood to rush to your skin's surface. When you switch the water to cold, the blood is rapidly moved away from the skin's surface towards the heart and internal organs. This process of moving blood towards the heart and away from the skin's surface, moves lymph fluid as well.

Jump on a rebounder (a mini-trampoline). When I was bed-ridden for several months due to a lymphatic disease, the only exercise I could do was rebound. Rebounding is a low-impact way to get blood and lymphatic fluid circulating throughout your body. It may seem like a simple thing, but just the rhythmic oscillation of the movement as you jump will help to move lymphatic fluid.

Start dry brushing. A dry brush (or skin brush) is a brush made with natural bristles, such as animal hair or vegetable fibers. With a dry brush, you massage your skin or "brush" it as much as you would your hair. Brush your skin towards your heart to get lymphatic fluid moving.

Get a massage. The massage therapist pushing on your body will stimulate lymphatic fluid movement.

Digestion and Mindset:

Your gut has been called the "second brain" by Dr. Michael Gershon, author of the book *The Second Brain: A Groundbreaking New Understanding of Nervous Disorders of the Stomach and Intestine*. Our gut is part of the enteric nervous system and contains around 100 million neurons. Our gut also contains the brain's feel-good chemicals, serotonin and dopamine. According to Dr. Pankaj Jay Pasricha, of the prestigious Stanford Hospital, over 90% of our body's serotonin and 50% of the body's dopamine are stored in the gut.

> **GORILLA MINDSET SHIFT:** IF IT'S GOOD FOR YOUR GUT, IT'S GOOD FOR YOUR BRAIN.

We all understand the relationship between our gut and our brain in real life. When we have an important event coming up, like a job interview, 5K race, or even a hot date, our bowels tend to act up on us. People who are nervous or worry often, complain about poor digestion. This is because your gut is a part of your nervous system—it "knows" your state of mind.

By now your digestion is likely improving due to the mindfulness and self-talk techniques you've learned here and are applying to your life. A mindful body is less stressed, and therefore, has better digestion. You can also improve your digestion by improving your diet. First, make sure you get enough fiber. Although experts disagree on the exact amount, I aim for around 30-40 grams of fiber each day. I eat a lot of high-fiber foods such as raspberries, oatmeal, air-popped popcorn (no butter), lentils, black and pinto beans, artichokes, Brussels sprouts, and even occasionally some Fiber Gummies (sugar-free gummy type candy available at Costco or Amazon.com).

You also have around 3-5 pounds of bacteria living in your gut. These bacteria can be harmful or helpful. The helpful bacteria are known as "probiotics." You can boost your probiotics by eating yogurt, kefir, and fermented foods like sauerkraut, or by taking an over-the-counter probiotic supplement. Related to probiotics are pre-biotics. Bacteria need food too, and their preferred food are pre-biotics. Pre-biotics come from fruit and green leafy vegetables, solid or juiced You can also take an over-the-counter supplement called Inulin.

As you can see, the mind-body connection is much deeper and more complex than you probably imagined. Everything is interconnected. Your posture, blood, digestion, diet and exercise, and your breathing all influence each other and work together as a whole. When any of these factors are out of balance, it can bring your whole body out of balance, which in turn puts your mindset out of balance.

Although you may not have heard about the lymphatic system, or perhaps you weren't aware of the "second brain," this is information that you should know about your body. It's not just theoretical knowledge. Your actionable take-away is simple:

- Exercise regularly.
- Move your body every day.
- Eat a diet of clean foods.
- Continue performing your Gorilla Mindset self-talk and mindfulness exercises.

When you're feeling unwell, you now know how to troubleshoot your own body.

The Gorilla Mindset Diet and Exercise Program:

If there was a Gorilla Mindset Diet and Exercise Program, the program would be based on these few general principles. If you apply them to your life, your health, fitness, and mindset will improve:

- Eat, blend, or juice 8-9 servings of vegetables and fruit each day.
- Lift weights 2-4 times per week.
- Perform cardio 3-5 times per week (can be alternated with lifting days).
- Do something physical every day (whether it's hiking, brisk walking, or even a massage).
- Avoid foods high in sugar, starch, or dairy.

Those principles leave open as many questions as they answer. What about protein? What about cheat meals? How many calories a day can I eat? As anyone who has spent as much time in the gym as I have has learned the answer is: "It depends." Some don't need as much protein as others. There are many vegans eating a solely plant-based diet with incredible physiques.

Some people can eat as much food as they want without gaining weight. Others can get fat just by looking at cheesecake. Unfortunately, we all have varying degrees of insulin sensitivity, which despite the terminology is a good trait to have. The more insulin sensitive you are, the more sugar and carbs you can eat. If you are insulin resistant, your body is more likely to store carbohydrates as fat. Go to GorillaMindset.com/Books if you'd like to explore these topics in greater detail.

Gorilla Mindset Optimal Foods:

Plants are the king of food. Diets high in plant foods are associated with every benefit you can imagine — lower cancer risk, higher cancer survival rates, a stronger immune system, and even better looking skin. Your diet should be based primarily around plants, and 8–9 servings of vegetables each day is an outstanding target to hit. Although all vegetables (and some fruit) are great choices, the best foods are those high on the ANDI index. The ANDI (short for Aggregate Nutrient Density Index) was created by Dr. Joel Fuhrman, M.D., a leading anti-aging physician.

Dr. Furhman attempted to quantify the best foods to eat based on the nutrient index of the foods. The ANDI score is based the amount of various plant nutrients and vitamins and minerals a food contains. The ANDI index also considers the free-radical fighting ability of foods. Collard greens, kale, spinach, brussel sprouts, arugula, red peppers, romaine lettuce, broccoli, and carrots are examples of commonly available foods that rate high on the ANDI index.

Get Your Greens:

Few of us eat enough vegetables. A popular alternative to munching on kale all day is to consume green juices and kale shakes, which provide 8-9 servings of fruits and vegetables. There is considerable controversy surrounding juicing. Most of the controversy is created by people who lack understanding of juicing. For example, some people say drinking a glass of apple juice can spike your blood sugar, creating blood sugar crashes.

I've written three books on juicing, and many of its advocates do not recommend high-sugar fruit juices. Instead, we recommend a base of kale, celery, cucumber, spinach and other leafy greens with a small amount of fruit added for sweetness and palatability. You can also make green smoothies. Joe Rogan, former host of *Fear Factor*, comedian, and UFC commentator, drinks a kale shake each morning. The "Joe Rogan Kale Shake," is a great way to supercharge your body with plant nutrients, while also providing a lot of fiber. Here's the recipe:

Joe Rogan Kale Shake:

- 4 stalks kale
- 4 celery stems
- 1 cucumber
- 1 pear
- ½ oz ginger (about the size of your thumb)
- 8 oz water (optional, helps items blend together smoothly).

Blend in a high-powered blender (with ice if preferred) and enjoy.

If you want to learn more about green juices or green smoothies, including several free recipes and tips, check out my website Fit-Juice.com. You can also find my books on juicing at Amazon.com.

Top 20 Foods for Health and Fitness:

The "Top 20" are foods that the fittest people tend to eat the most of that are ranked high on the ANDI scale. These foods are chosen for their high anti-oxidant profile, alkalinity, or because they are low in sugar and high in nutrients.

The 20 best foods to base your diet around are:

- Chicken
- Salmon
- White fish
- Lean beef
- Kale
- Carrots
- Sweet or white potatoes
- Rice
- Eggs (eat those yolks, they're good for you)
- Blueberries
- Brussels sprouts
- Arugula
- Red peppers
- Romaine lettuce
- Broccoli
- Asparagus
- Spinach
- Tomatoes
- Oranges

Of course, you can eat a wide variety of food, but if you build your diet around these 20 foods, you will enjoy a high level of health and aesthetic physique.

How Many Calories Should You Eat Per Day:

It's impossible to say in the abstract how many calories a person should eat each day, as daily caloric intake is based on factors like overall muscle mass, activity level, and basal metabolic rate (how "fast" your resting metabolism is). Bodyweight (in pounds) x 15 is a good starting point if you go to the gym 3-4 times each week and perform cardio, hike, or otherwise engage in a lot of other physical activity. For example, a 200-pound man could consume 3,500 kcals a day without gaining fat. Bodyweight x 13-14 is a good starting point if you don't work a physically demanding job and train at the gym 3-4 times each week. For example, a 180-pound male could eat 2,340 to 2,500 kcals a day without gaining any fat.

Again, those numbers will vary individually. When you're first starting off, track your daily caloric intake with some software like FitDay, a free online food and nutrient tracking program. It allows you to track your activity, bodyweight, and daily caloric intake. Weigh yourself while tracking your food to learn how many calories you can eat in a day.

How Many Grams of Protein, Carbohydrate, and Fat Should You Eat Per Day:

I recommend following the isocaloric diet or *Zone Diet*. Under both you eat approximately the same number of calories from protein, carbohydrates, and fat. I tend to balance my calories between protein, carbohydrates, and fat, while others prefer more carbohydrates. (The less insulin sensitive you are, the less carbohydrates you can eat.) When you track your macronutrients (or "macros"), you'll figure out what works best for you. Keep track of everything when starting out. It's tedious at first, but eventually you'll be able to eat more instinctively. As with everything else, eating well becomes more automatic the more you practice it. I don't monitor my food at all anymore, as I have a good sense of what my body's needs are. However, when I started out, I weighed myself and my food, daily, and tracked every meal. Now I can coast, but that is only because I put in the hard work early on.

How Often Should You Eat:

This is another question that doesn't have a "one size fits all" answer, and in fact, it causes a lot of controversy. Some people believe you must eat every 2-3 hours to keep your blood sugar levels regulated. Others argue you needn't eat nearly so often and recommend intermittent fasting. I use intermittent fasting on a 16-8 split. That is, I fast throughout each day for 16 hours. Then I eat in an 8-hour window. I started off by eating every 12 hours on, 12 hours off. I worked myself up to 16-18 hour fasts. Others need more frequent feedings. Try it out to see what works for you.

Mike's Sample Day of Eating and Lifting:

- Wake up at 8 a.m.
- Drink coffee or green tea.
- Have my first meal of eggs, vegetables, and lean meat at 2 p.m.
- Go to the gym at 3 p.m.
- Drink a juice with protein powder after lifting.
- Eat a reasonable meal containing some of the "Top 20 Foods" from above around 6pm.
- Eat another reasonable meal, along with some 85% dark chocolate around 8pm.

I realize this section opens as many questions as it answers. For several books you can read to learn more, go to GorillaMindset.com/Books.

Bonus Interview with Dr. Brett Osborn, DO, FAANS, CSCS

To ensure the information presented here is the most accurate and up to date, I consulted experts such as Dr. Brett Osborn, DO, FAANS, CSCS. Dr. Osborn is a Board-Certified Neurosurgeon with a secondary certification in Anti-Aging and Regenerative Medicine. He is the proverbial "brain surgeon."

Dr. Osborn also takes health and fitness seriously, believing that exercise is the best preventative medicine available. Dr. Osborn wrote a book about health and fitness called *Get Serious*, which I recommend at GorillaMindset.com/Books.

I was fortunate enough to be able to talk health, fitness, and mindset with him, you can read the interview below:

Mike Cernovich: Dr. Osborn, thanks for joining me. As you know, there are countless books on diet and exercise making bold promises. What drew me to your book *Get Serious* is its overall approach to health and fitness. Your attitude is not simply that we should lift weights and exercise to look good, but because it's healthy for us.

Dr. Brett Osborn: Exactly. I do not view health and fitness as a personal trainer might. I view health and fitness from a doctor's perspective.

I stress throughout my book, and in consultations with patients, that health and fitness is a lifestyle choice impacting all areas of health. Lifting weights and exercising is the best preventive medicine available.

Mike Cernovich: How does exercise improve our physical health?

Dr. Brett Osborn: I cover the physiological mechanisms in details in *Get Serious*. When lifting weights, you force your body to undergo a short-term stress. Some people believe all stress is bad. In fact, our bodies evolved to respond favorably to stress — if it's the right kind of stress.

Exercise has an anti-inflammatory response, as your body produces substances to help deal with the short-term inflammation caused by exercising. Although we think inflammation is bad, it's the chronic long-term inflammation that is harmful. Short-term inflammation from a vigorous training session is highly beneficial for your overall health.

The 4-5 hours a week you spend in the gym leaves your body with less inflammation than do the other 168 hours.

Mike Cernovich: You also write that exercise reduces our chances of contracting certain diseases. How so?

Dr. Brett Osborn: Yes, in addition to boosting our immune systems, which helps our bodies fight off general illness, exercise can prevent many of the lifestyle diseases plaguing the West.

Resistance training improves glucose tolerance, making one less likely to develop Type II diabetes. Resistance training also improves cardiovascular function, increases HDL (the "good cholesterol") levels, and boosts the immune system by encouraging lymphatic fluid flow.

Mike Cernovich: What other benefits does exercise have?

Dr. Brett Osborn: How much time do we have?! We could talk about the benefits of exercise for hours, as they are countless. For example, numerous studies have shown critically ill patients with higher levels of muscle mass are more likely to survive than those with less muscle mass. Moreover, a 2008 study published in the British Medical Journal showed muscular strength is inversely and independently associated with death from all causes and cancer in men, even after adjusting for cardiorespiratory fitness.

Mike Cernovich: You stress the importance of strength and weight training, why is that?

Dr. Brett Osborn: Muscle is not something only people who want to look a certain way should care about. Muscle matters to everyone.

Muscle serves a structural role in your body. Muscle supports our skeletal system, our joints and ligaments. Around 44 million Americans have low bone mineral density. By training with weights, they can improve bone density, leading to fewer fractures.

Lifting weights can also improve posture and strengthen the lower back, which is the major cause of work-related injuries.

Mike Cernovich: While I know you're not a psychologist, you have a deep understanding of the brain. Would you say lifting weights also improves our mental health and cognitive function?

Dr. Brett Osborn: Yes. Risk factors for cerebrovascular diseases are not different than those for cardiovascular disease. Exercise has been shown to alter the progression of Alzheimer's and Parkinson's disease. These benefits are thought to be due to the antioxidant effect of exercise and improved blood flow.

Our brains demand up to 25% of the blood flowing through our body. Exercise improves blood flow and heart function, leading to more efficient blood flow to the brain. Exercise has also been shown to reduce stress.

As I write in *Get Serious*, "*Therefore, at the cellular level, exercise 'works' the brain. Synapses are formed and connections to the peripheral nervous system are reinforced. By acquiring the skills you need to exercise a squat or dead lift, you are creating neural pathways.*" In other words, working out the body works out the mind.

Mike Cernovich: What type of exercise should a person who wants to improve his overall health and mindset undertake?

Dr. Brett Osborn: Strength training, that is, exercising with weights. Lifting weights improves your muscular structure, boosts your immune system, and does not provide excess stress hormones like cortisol (which running and other long-duration cardio can do).

Mike Cernovich: Does that mean we shouldn't perform any "cardio" at all?

Dr. Brett Osborn: Shorter duration cardio is beneficial. Interval training (that is, where you perform an all-out effort like a sprint for 20-30 seconds followed by 60-90 seconds of low-intensity movement) is helpful for fat loss and overall health. High intensity interval training also increases blood flow to all parts of the body, including the brain.

Mike Cernovich: I hate to put you on the spot, but someone is sure to ask, "What if I only have time to do cardio or lift? What should I do?"

Dr. Brett Osborn: Without question, lift weights. I would rather see a healthy person do 50 bodyweight squats a day than walk one mile.

Time management is a challenge for all of us, and with the demands of modern life, it's easy to say we "don't have time" to exercise. But this is your health.

Make time for taking control of your health today or your body will force you to make time to recover from illness and disease in the future.

Mike Cernovich: Thanks so much for taking the time to talk to us. Your comments were insightful and show why everyone — even people who aren't "vain" — should be lifting weights. Where can we learn more about you?

Dr. Brett Osborn: Check out my book *Get Serious*. I talk about the exact mechanisms we discussed here in more detail. I also lay out a sample diet and exercise plan.

Dr. Osborn is an NYU-trained Board-Certified Neurological Surgeon (ABNS) with a secondary certification in Anti-Aging and Regenerative Medicine. He has also earned the CSCS honorarium from the National Strength and Conditioning Association (NSCA). In addition to spending the last ten-plus post-residency years performing over 1,500 brain and spine operations, he has counseled an equal number of patients on the roles of sound nutrition and exercise in their quest for total body health. Dr. Osborn practices in Jupiter, FL.

Top Health and Fitness Tips:

> **GORILLA MINDSET SHIFT:** YOU ONLY HAVE ONE BODY. TAKE CARE OF IT, AS IT HAS TO LAST YOUR ENTIRE LIFE.

The 80/20 rule (which says you receive 80% of your results from 20% of your activity) applies to your health and fitness goals. Rather than stress and agonize over every gram of food you eat, whether you're doing the "best" workout at the gym or following the "perfect" diet, focus on what matters. Go to the gym. Lift weights. Do some cardio afterwards. That one hour you spend in the gym is what's going to carry you through the other 23 hours of your day.

Lifting weights is the single best habit you can add to your life to improve your health, fitness and aesthetics. Lifting weights is superior to all other forms of exercise, as the amount of muscle mass you carry is related to how long you live, how often you get sick, and how quickly your body recovers from injury or illness. Weight lifting also boosts bone mineral density, which is especially important as you age. Two great books offering detailed training instructions include *Body of a Spartan* and *Becoming the Bull*.

The best brain-boosting drug (or nootropic) on the market is exercise. As neuroscientist Prof. Sam Wang states in his book, *The Great Courses: The Neuroscience of Everyday Life*, "*If something is good for the heart, it's good for the brain.*" Exercise boosts blood flow to your brain, improving circulation and thus, making you more intelligent while improving your memory.

The leaner you are, the more carbohydrates you can eat. Carbohydrates are less likely to be stored as fat if your body fat percentage is low. If you can pinch fat around your waist, you should err on the side of keeping your carbs lower. Aim for under 30% of your daily caloric intake from carbs.

You can combine protein and fat, protein and carbs, and protein and carbs and fat. You cannot combine fat and carbs together without protein, as that causes the body to secrete excess insulin and store the food as fat. Always eat some protein with your carbs and fat. If you're going to eat a large holiday meal, birthday dinner, or other special occasion meal (or even if you feel you're about to binge eat), consume as much broccoli or other low-calorie, high volume foods. This will leave you satiated and mitigate any harm you might otherwise do to your body. Also, the added fiber from the food will help your body process the fat from the unhealthy food before it's digested and stored as fat.

You can also mitigate the dietary harm of a binge meal or cheat day by using fiber tablets, fiber powder, or even Fiber Gummies. (They are sweet, sugar-free fiber chews that look and taste like gummy bears.) Dietary fiber lowers your body's insulin response to food, as it slows digestion. Fiber also can bind to fat from the meal, carrying it through your body to be eliminated before being stored.

The post-workout window is overhyped, but real. According to the theory of nutrient timing, which was researched by Dr. John Ivy, a professor and head of the Department of Kinesiology, the body will preferentially use calories consumed immediately after a hard training session for growth and repair of muscle tissue, rather than store the nutrients as body fat. It's overhyped in the sense that bodybuilding magazines sell you exotic supplements to increase the gains. It's real in the sense that you can eat most any type of food you want after a hard lifting session without getting fat. Use some judgment and don't eat an entire pizza, but even two slices of pizza after a hard lifting session, while not optimal, won't hurt your progress.

Note: Yoga, cardio, or anything not involving hardcore lifting does not count as the post-workout window. People often slurp down 800 calorie smoothies after Yoga or 30 minutes on the treadmill, taking two steps back in their fitness goals.

If you're worried about the "sugar" in juice, then drink your juice before, during, or after you lift weights. I drink beet juice before lifting, as beet juice boosts athletic performance better than any supplement on the market.

The best time to do cardio is whenever you get a chance to do it. There is much debate in the fitness community as to whether you should do cardio first thing in the morning on an empty stomach, after you lift weights, or at some other time. That is much ado about nothing. Doing your cardio is what matters and you won't notice a difference one way or another.

We are food addicts. Modern processed food is made to be addicting. Scientists engineer the most minute details of food, including creating special grains of salt that hit your tongue in a specific way to maximize the taste of the food. Avoid processed foods as much as possible, as it's very difficult to maintain an optimal level of health while eating a diet high in processed foods.

Break your fat loss goal into parts. It can seem demoralizing having 80 pounds of fat to lose. I know, as I lost 80 pounds of fat, going from a high of 260 pounds to a bodyweight of 180. Yet I looked and felt better after losing the first 20 pounds. I could have framed my progress as, "Oh man I have another 60 to lose!" Remember to use the power of the reframing. Remind yourself that you will look better after losing 20 pounds, even better after losing 20 more, and before you know it you will have met your fat-loss goal.

Yes, you can eat after 6 p.m. However, you should keep your carbohydrate intake low, as the body does not process carbohydrates well at night. A common late night snack for me is a hand full of almonds and a scoop of protein powder with almond milk, eggs, or egg whites.

You're going to have highs and lows in your fitness journey. You're going to have great workouts, mediocre workouts, and sometimes you're going to ask yourself, "Why bother?" Remember the Gorilla Mindset Shift. One body, one life. Life has highs and lows, and your health and fitness progress will be no different. Do not stress out over one bad workout or plateau. Progress in the gym, and in general, is non-linear. We seem to make little progress for weeks, or even months, and then notice drastic improvement.

How can you stay motivated to go to the gym? First, go to the gym. Afterwards you'll feel refreshed and your body will release endorphins and other feel-good chemicals. Write out how you felt after your workout and use our mental state-control techniques to capture the feeling. Then, when you don't feel like lifting weights, return to the moment where you felt energized after working out and you'll feel motivated to go to the gym.

GORILLA MINDSET SHIFT: NO MATTER HOW YOU FEEL BEFORE GOING TO THE GYM, YOU WILL ALWAYS FEEL BETTER AFTERWARDS.

GORILLA FITNESS HABITS

1. Throw Away All Junk Food

"Out of sight, out of mind." Make it hard to eat unhealthy foods.

2. Avoid All "White Foods," Including Sugar, Milk, and Bread

While milk and bread are not necessarily bad for everyone, many people have trouble with those foods. Right now, you want to focus on this one simple rule. Cut these foods out for a month. You can always reintroduce them to see if and how they affect you.

3. Focus on What You *Can* Eat

Instead of viewing clean healthy eating as depriving yourself, focus on the foods you *can* eat, which are myriad. Focusing on what you *can* have, rather than what you can't is essential to establishing an abundance mindset. There is a huge list of tasty nutritious foods in the previous section. Focus on ways to spice them up, rather than feeling deprived.

4. Buy a Spice Rack

Spices are high in anti-oxidants and will help you avoid getting bored when eating healthy foods. You can only eat so many eggs before it gets boring. Throw on some curry powder, and suddenly you have a new meal.

5. Get a Crock Pot

A crock pot will turn even the leanest, flavorless meat into a juicy tasty meal. A crock pot is also great because you can cook your food efficiently. I turn my crock pot on in the morning before work, set the it to low temperature, and return home 8-10 hours later to a great meal (and my house smells wonderful too!).

6. Start Juicing (or Blending)

Green juices and smoothies are a great way to fulfill your body's need for nutrients. Often when you feel hungry, your body is really telling you it's undernourished. To learn more about juicing, go to FitJuice.com or check out my juicing book, *Juice Power*, on Amazon.

TOP 10 MINDSET SUPPLEMENTS:

Nutritional supplements have received a bad rap for two reasons. First, we are skeptical about supplements because bodybuilding magazines, which are full of steroid-using fitness models, make outrageous and fraudulent claims about the efficacy of supplements. Second, the supplement industry is unregulated, which is a double-edged sword. On one hand, this means many supplement companies do not put into their product what the label claims. On the other hand, valuable, life-saving supplements can get to market faster since 7-year long FDA trials are not required before they can be released.

As you now know, mindset and health are linked. These supplements will improve your mindset by increasing blood flow to your brain, reducing free radical damage, helping regulate your blood sugar and more. These supplements will improve health and mental clarity, but remember, they are only supplements, something extra you add to your overall healthy lifestyle. For a complete listing of the supplements I recommend, check out GorillaMindset.com/Supplements.

Below is a list of the 10 best supplements I recommend, but first, I'd like to go over some of the most common concerns people have when adding supplements to their daily routine.

Which Supplement Companies Can You Trust:

Since supplements are unregulated, I suggest using only these most reputable brands:

- Jarrow
- Life Extension
- NOW Foods
- Advanced Orthomolecular Research (AOR)
- Costco's brand "Kirkland"

These brands have all been scrutinized by watch dog groups like Consumer Reports and their supplements contain what the label claims.

How to Supplement Safely and Effectively:

Some supplements work better than others. Trial and error is the name of the game. What works well for you might do little for me, and vice versa. For me, magnesium is a game changer. I used to get restless leg syndrome, which kept me up at night. Taking magnesium has eliminated the symptoms. A reader also wrote in telling me he cured his insomnia of three years after he took my suggestion and began taking epsom salt baths (which is a good source of magnesium).

Should You Take a Mulit-Vitamin:

Again, since the supplement industry is unregulated, most multi-vitamins do not contain an effective dose of vitamins and minerals. There are, however, three multi-vitamins that provide concentrated amounts of essential vitamins and minerals. AOR Ortho Core, the Life Extension Foundation's Life Extension Mix, and Super Nutrition Opti-Pak, are all excellent multivitamins. Do read the labels, however, as some multivitamins contain a version of vitamin B3 that causes what's known as the *niacin rush*, or reddening and flushing of the skin lasting 10-20 minutes.

Consult Your Physician Before Starting Any Supplements:

Some supplements may be contraindicated for certain conditions. For example, fish oil and aspirin may be contraindicated in cases where someone has a blood-clotting condition. Always disclose your supplement use to your physician.

Now, are you ready for that top 10 list? Here we go:

1. N-A-C: N-acetylcysteine boosts levels of glutathione in the body. Glutathione is a powerful liver detoxifier. Many illnesses, like depression and anxiety, are understood now as being caused by free radical damage, rather than chemical imbalances or low serotonin.

At the end of this chapter, I'll go into more detail about how I used N-A-C to treat mild symptoms of depression and anxiety. One reader emailed telling me his father's unyielding depression was finally under control after he read my N-A-C article, and began taking it. Many others have also reached out telling me N-A-C improved their symptoms of anxiety and depression.

I suggest taking 2 grams of N-A-C in divided doses (one gram twice each day), preferably on an empty stomach.

2. ZMA (Zinc and Magnesium): Magnesium is responsible for over 500 different biological processes. Suboptimal levels of magnesium lead to heart disease, depression, restless leg syndrome, and even insomnia.

Magnesium can also be absorbed through the skin. A warm bath with 1-2 cups of epsom salt is a relaxing, effective way to realize the benefits of magnesium. Zinc boosts your immune system, improves endothelial function, and can even boost testosterone levels. ZMA is an easy way to take adequate amounts of both supplements at once. I take 50 mg of zinc and 500 mg of magnesium before bed on an empty stomach. When sweating a lot, I take up to 1,000 mg of magnesium.

3. Vitamin D3: Vitamin D is a hormone responsible for bone health, heart function, and mood. Most people are deficient in Vitamin D, as the natural source of Vitamin D is the sun. Most of us avoid the sun, or when we do go out, we wear sunscreen. Seasonal Affective Disorder (SAD) is due to low levels of sunlight, and Vitamin D3 has been used to help treat symptoms of depression. Some research suggests that Vitamin D may also have anti-cancer properties. I take 5,000IU of Vitamin D a day with a meal.

4. Fish oil: Inflammation is a killer, and fish oil is anti-inflammatory. Some believe those living in "blue zones" (areas with the highest concentration of people who lived to be over 100 years of age) owe their longevity to a high intake of fatty fish. Most doctors consider fish oil a must-have supplement, and Dr. Brett Obsorn, the neurosurgeon and anti-aging physician you met earlier in the book, advises everyone without contradictions take between 5 and 15 grams of fish oil daily. My preferred way of ingesting fish oil is drinking lemon-flavored Carlson's Fish Oil. I actually like the lemon-flavor and can drink a shot right out of the bottle. There are also tablets, which are much less likely to cause "fish oil burps," a common but mild side effect of taking fish oil. I take 5-10 grams of fish oil daily.

5. Greens+: Eating your vegetables or making green juices and smoothies is the best step you can take for your overall health. Yet we often travel, making it impractical to get in enough greens. That's where a greens powder like Greens+ is helpful.

Greens+ is an acquired taste. The Wild Berry Greens+ is much more palatable to new users. I take 1-2 servings daily.

6. Whey protein: Protein from whole food sources like lean meat, chicken, salmon, eggs, and lentils is optimal. Yet it's hard to take in adequate amounts of protein. Whey protein is more of a food source in my view. It's a quick and tasty way to get in extra protein. Peptides in whey protein boost the immune system. I take 25-50 grams of whey protein a day.

7. Curcumin: Curcumin is a compound isolated from turmeric. Curcumin reduces inflammation throughout the body and is also used to treat inflammatory conditions like rheumatoid arthritis. Some research suggests that curcumin can slow the growth of cancerous tumors. Ordinary curcumin is hard for the body to absorb, and thus many products contain piperine, an alkaloid found in black pepper, that makes curcumin more bioavailable. I take 500 to 1,000 mg of curcumin with piperine daily.

8. B-Complex (B vitamins): B vitamins include thiamine, riboflavin, B3 (niacin), B6, B12, and folic acid. B vitamins improve heart and nerve health and are commonly added to "energy drinks" to improve clarity, mood, and concentration. Low levels of B vitamins in the body lead to anemia, low energy, and poor memory. My preferred B-complex is made by a niche Canadian company known as AOR. Their B-complex contains methylcobalamin, which is the more bioavilable version of B12. I take 1 to 3 B-complex tablets on an empty stomach, usually first thing in the morning, and then another in early afternoon.

9. Nootropics: As mentioned earlier, the best nootropic is exercise. Many "brain boosting supplements" offer a lot of hype while delivering little results. There are, however, two nootropics with considerable research behind them:

- ***Vinpocetine*** is a supplement extracted from the periwinkle plant that has been shown to improve blood flow to the brain. As you saw in earlier sections, more blood to the brain improves cognition and enhances memory. Vinpocetine may also help prevent strokes, again due to its ability to increase blood flow. 10-20 mgs of vinpocetine does the trick for me, although I don't use it every day.

- ***Piracetam*** is an anti-clotting supplement that increases blood flow through the body and has even been shown to help treat deep-vein thrombosis. By now, I may be sounding like a broken record, but the pattern cannot be overstated. Activities and supplements that improve blood flow improve overall health and cognition.

10. Mood-Enhancement Supplements Some supplements have been shown to help improve and ease symptoms of anxiety and depression through regulating serotonin. Unlike the other supplements mentioned above, these do not work by improving blood flow, but rather by helping the body better regulate serotonin, a "feel good chemical" the body produces. Low serotonin leads to sadness, and in many cases, severe depression.

- ***Tryptophan*** is an essential amino acid, as the body cannot produce it on its own. Tryptophan is a precursor to serotonin, meaning the body produces serotonin from tryptophan. Results with tryptophan vary person to person, but the average dose is 500 to 2,000 mg daily.

- ***5-HTP*** has been shown in several studies to be an effective form of treating depression, as 5-HTP is another serotonin precursor. 5-HTP is also an effective sleep aid, as it can reduce symptoms of anxiety. I take 100 to 500 mg of 5-HTP when undergoing extensive stress or having difficulty sleeping.

For more information about supplements, including the best places to purchase them, go to GorillaMindset.com/Supplements

How I Used N-A-C to Conquer Depression:

I used to get depressed and feel anxious. I never had full-on panic attacks, but I had severe anxiety that would leave my brain spinning and my skin would break out in rashes.

I conquered my anxiety through two means, as anxiety and depression have two components — physical and psychological. The psychological component of anxiety come from social pressures and the feeling that if you do not live up to the expectations of others, then you are not good enough. That is why mental state control, reframing, and other Gorilla Mindset techniques calm your mind.

The physical components of anxiety and depression come from a variety of sources, such as poor nutrition, lack of sunlight, excessive oxidative stress, high cortisol, and heavy metal poisoning.

N-Acetylcysteine (N-A-C) has been clinically proven to help treat symptoms of anxiety and depression.

N-Acetylcysteine is a powerful nootropic with many benefits and has been used by visionary doctors to help treat persistant depression and anxiety.

Why haven't you heard about the magical effects of N-A-C? Simple. Go to Amazon.com and see how much a bottle of N-A-C costs. My mom was on a $1,500 a month cocktail of drugs. No one would listen when I suggested they buy a $15 bottle of N-A-C. But the science is there. As noted in *N-acetyl cysteine for depressive symptoms in bipolar disorder–a double-blind randomized placebo-controlled trial*: "NAC appears to be a safe and effective augmentation strategy for depressive symptoms in bipolar disorder." See also *N-acetyl cysteine as a glutathione precursor for schizophrenia–a double-blind, randomized, placebo-controlled trial*: "This data suggests that adjunctive NAC has potential as a safe and moderately effective augmentation strategy for chronic schizophrenia."

How N-A-C Helps Treat Depression:

Acetylcysteine is a glutathione precursor. That is, acetylcysteine is converted into glutathione. Glutathione is an antioxidant that used by your liver to detox your body. Emergency rooms give high doses of NAC to patients that have overdosed with Tylenol.

The Relation Between Mental Illness and the Liver:

Could mental illness be caused by toxins that your liver is unable to eliminate from the body due to glutathione deficiency? It's not so far-fetched, in fact, the cutting-edge of mental health research is looking at the role toxins and oxidative stress play in mental illness.

In *The efficacy of adjunctive N-acetylcysteine in major depressive disorder: a double-blind, randomized, placebo-controlled trial* "This data implicates the pathways influenced by NAC in depression pathogenesis, principally oxidative and inflammatory stress and glutamate, although definitive confirmation remains necessary." See also, *The Glutathione System: A New Drug Target in Neuroimmune Disorders* "Glutathione depletion and concomitant increase in oxidative and neurological stress and mitochondrial dysfunctions play a role in the pathophysiology of diverse neuroimmune disorders, including depression, myalgic encephalomyelitis/chronic fatigue syndrome and Parkinson's disease, suggesting that depleted GSH is an integral part of these diseases."

How Much N-A-C Should You Take:

That would be medical advice, which I cannot give. However, participants in the studies used between 1 and 2 grams daily.

Why Take N-A-C Instead of Glutathione:

If N-A-C is a precursor, wouldn't it make more sense to take glutathione directly? That seems logical, but evidence suggests that N-A-C is more bioavailable than glutathione. I personally use N-A-C because that was the compound studied. How much glutathione would one need to take to get the same benefits that one can obtain from 1 to 2 grams of N-A-C? I don't know, as I went with N-A-C. You are free to try both for yourself to see what works best for you. Please let me know what you discover.

CHAPTER 8

Mindset and Posture: How Posture Affects Your Physical and Mental Health

Your body and mind, as I hope you now appreciate more than ever, are not separate entities. They are linked. Moreover, your posture impacts your mood, feeling of well-being, and even your hormonal levels.

Improving your posture will improve your state of mind, so I've included several detailed pictures of proper posture in this chapter. First, I'd like to share another conversation I had with Dr. Jeremy Nicholson on the scientific basis for how posture relates to mindset:

Mike Cernovich: Dr Nicholson, we've talked before about the importance of posture. My back-of-the-envelope theory is that strong posture is important and associated with exuding confidence and a more dominant stature. In a primal environment, the primates who took up the most space had the most status. What is your view on posture?

Dr. Jeremy Nicholson: Much of what you suggest has been supported for 30 years or more by research on primates (including us humans).

For example, in 1985 Mazer published an article discussing how biology, behavior, and social status interact in primate groups. The summary of that paper says:

This paper describes a biosocial model of status in face-to-face groups. It argues that status ranks are allocated among members of a group through face-to-face interaction and that the allocation process is similar across each primate species, including humans. Every member of a group signifies its rank through physical or vocal demeanor. For example, behavioral signs of dominant status include erect posture, glares, eye contact, strutting, and (in humans) assertive speech. Individuals whose behaviors exhibit dominance show high or rising levels of testosterone compared to those who exhibit deference. Testosterone and dominance are reciprocally related. The model relies more on research on males than females. It is proposed as a theory about both sexes, but with a caution that little is known about sex differences in the relation of hormones to dominance behavior.

Essentially then, dominant behaviors, status or power in a social group, and testosterone levels all reciprocally influence one another.

Mike Cernovich: Does the research support my claim that better posture can naturally increase testosterone levels?

Dr. Nicholson: Yes.

1. Good posture itself may have an effect. Having an open, upright, and relaxed posture may simply help the body function overall. At the least, such postures can promote relaxation, which decreases stress hormones like cortisol, and can therefore increase testosterone. A study by Carney, Cuddy, and Yap (2010), which I mentioned in the article about the science of posture and testosterone, did find a reduction in cortisol for participants who posed in powerful postures. Therefore, the effect Mike is getting with these exercises may be some kind of structural alignment, or even a relaxation response type of phenomenon.

2. Dominant body language also has a reciprocal relationship with emotions. For example, when we are happy, we smile. BUT, if we force ourselves to hold a smile, we will also become

happier (Zajonc, Murphy, & Inglehart, 1989). In much the same way as a smile affects mood, powerful body language may also be helping to create positive emotions and an assertive mindset. In support of that idea, the study I cited above by Carney, Cuddy, and Yap (2010) also found that participants striking high power postures felt significantly more powerful and in charge, compared to low power posturing peers, and were also more focused on rewards.

Such psychological states, in turn, may relate to other neuroendocrine changes. Thus, we may also be seeing a "fake it until you make it" type effect on mindset and emotion, leading to greater testosterone production as well.

In either case, the main benefit of such postures is that they can be done routinely and constantly.

Practicing such body language and mindset can result in them being chronically activated. Therefore, rather than getting a temporary increase from a workout or a victory, such exercises may allow for regulation of testosterone over a longer time frame. After all, the research I discussed in the science of posture and testosterone article about changes in testosterone levels in men during marriage and divorce, seems to indicate longer-term effects on testosterone due to psychological and social changes (Mazur & Booth, 1998).

In short, the added benefit of these exercises may come from the fact that they help to relax the body, promote good behavioral habits, and/or improve mindset and emotions — which better regulate testosterone levels over the long term. In other words, this is not simply "performing an exercise", but rather developing the habit of functioning in a physiologically and psychologically powerful and masculine way.

Of course, all of this is an educated hypothesis, based on the results of other studies. Additional testing would be necessary to tease apart a more specific "why" among these reciprocal relationships.

Mike's personal results, however, certainly serve as a good case study to support that these longer-term effects are taking place by at least one of these paths, if not more.

Mike Cernovich: That's fascinating. Thank you for taking time to talk with me. By the way, do you have any references, as I'm sure some people would love to read more?

Dr. Nicholson: Yes, I do.

References:

- Carney, D.R., Cuddy, A.J.C., Yap, A.J. (2010). Power posing: Brief nonverbal displays affect neuroendocrine levels and risk tolerance. Psychological Science, 21, 1363-1368.
- Mazer, A. (1985). A biosocial model of status in face-to-face primate groups. Social Forces, 64, 377-402.
- Mazur, A., & Booth, A. (1998). Testosterone and dominance in men. Behavioral and Brain Sciences, 21, 353-397.
- Zajonc, R. B., Murphy, S. T. & Inglehart, M. (1989). Feeling and facial efference: Implications for the vascular theory of emotion. Psychological Review, 96, 395-416.

Poor Posture: Causes and Cures

Poor posture results from repetition, largely due to the pressures, temptations, and distractions of the modern world. Even my own posture can be terrible and I'm always working to improve it. As I work online, my shoulders suffer from forward pronation (too far forward), leading to pain.

When working at a desk or on my laptop, I have the same bad posture habits you likely have. Most of us develop poor posture from using our smartphones. It even has a name, which my friend

Victor Pride introduced me to: *iPosture* — the posture caused by our iPhones.

After sitting for hours each day at our desk or with our portable electronic devices, our posture looks terrible.

This is posture we often see in ourselves and others:

This is proper posture:

You can improve your posture, but just as improving your mindset takes time, correcting bad posture is not something you will achieve overnight. These exercises require vigilance. Expect to see gradual improvement rather than overnight results.

We have trained our bodies to have poor posture. It can take months to unlearn the bad habit. As physical therapists often say, "You can't undo 23 hours of bad posture with one hour a day in the gym."

Perform these posture exercises as often as you can. I do one to two sets of 10 reps throughout the day, as posture is something I am consistently training.

You may feel some tightness since your muscles are not used to the stretches. You may also experience coughing, since poor posture also allows excess carbon dioxide to be trapped in your lungs, which your body expels as part of the respiratory process. Also, your diaphragm is compressed when your posture is poor, leading to poor breathing.

The Abundance Posture:

The abundance posture pose opens your hips, shoulders, pelvis, and abs. You may even cough or feel pulling in your stomach area. That's your abdominal cavity. Those muscles have been compressed due to sitting, which presses the muscle fibers against one another.

There are three parts to the abundance posture pose. Although these are three separate pictures, you'll do the movements as fluidly as possible.

Step 1. While standing with your legs slightly more than shoulder width apart, thrust your butt while raising your chest up. Your arms may hang freely by your sides like this:

Step 2. Extend your arms up in the air and imagine yourself opening your body up to the world. As you raise your arms, feel your chest and neck start to rise up and backward behind you:

Step 3. As you perform this movement more fluidly, you'll start to feel yourself fall backwards. Your arms are reaching back behind you, almost as if you are about to fall. You should feel your abdominal muscles and hips opening fully:

The Abundance Posture Pose should be performed frequently. I do 5-10 reps several times each day.

How to Improve Your Posture While Standing:

Sitting makes our hips tighten and shoulders to become pronated. Perform the following exercises to help bring your shoulders back into proper alignment.

Stand up against the wall with your posture as perfect as possible, keeping your arms pressed up against the wall.

Face the wall carefully, then extend your arms out as widely as you can. Really feel your shoulders open up.

Face the wall with your triceps parallel to the ground and your forearms perpendicular to the wall. Hold this position for 15 seconds.

How to Improve Your Posture While Sitting:

You can perform a variation of the Abundance Posture Pose while sitting. As with the exercise above, you want to focus on raising your chest, opening up your abs, and stretching your arms.

Sit with your triceps parallel to the ground and forearms perpendicular to the ground. Hold this position for 15-30 seconds.

Extend your arms out as widely as you can, again opening up your chest. Imagine you are looking up at something that is above and slightly behind you.

You can find these posture exercises and more at: GorillaMindset.com/Posture

The page is password protected and exclusive to those who have purchased this *Gorilla Mindset* book.

The password is Cernovich (case-sensitive).

CHAPTER 9

MINDSET AND MONEY: HOW TO KEEP MONEY IN PERSPECTIVE AND IN YOUR POCKET

There's a lot to learn about mindset and money – too many details to cover here. This overview will help you start thinking intelligently about money by reframing how you think about it, and thus, your relationship with it. We'll discuss ways you can earn more money by thinking of yourself as a corporation and how to save money on taxes while investing intelligently.

> **GORILLA MINDSET SHIFT:** "MONEY IS LIKE OXYGEN. WITHOUT IT YOU WILL DIE."

Money is not just something you want, it is something you need. Without money, it is simply impossible to live. Yet somewhere along the way we were taught that money is evil.

My relationship with money is complicated. Growing up poor, I had no conception of what money was or how people made it. I believed that you had to steal from people to make a lot of money. I was also afraid to believe in myself enough to take the risks requires to hit it big. My relationship with money changed during college, and I have never looked back.

"Yo, Cerno, can I borrow your car," a friend of mine asked. "Sure thing, just get it back to me at the end of the day." I replied. I had an old Ford Escort station wagon, which got me from point A to point B.

You can see how this story ends. Yes, my friend crashed my car.

Whether it was my friend's fault or not was irrelevant. My car was totaled and beyond repair. I felt powerless and hopeless. I needed a car to drive to work, as public transportation wasn't available. A girl who lived in a nearby apartment drove me to work and I thought to myself, "This will be the last time I never have money again."

GORILLA MINDSET SHIFT: MONEY IS NEITHER GOOD NOR EVIL.

The pursuit of money is far from the root of all evil. Having money allows you to do good in the world. Having money allows you to avoid compromising your values. Money gives you access to better food, better healthcare, and more charity.

Here's an experiment: Make a lot of money and if you decide having money is a bad thing, give it all away. What you'll find after making a lot of money is that you can do a lot of good in the world. For example, I was able to produce a free podcast in my spare time as a lawyer. The money I made from practicing law helped me change countless lives.

On a grander scale, the New York Public Library — and in fact the entire U.S. Library system — was founded and funded by those who relentlessly pursued money.

You can make money honestly and ethically. You can use your money to do good in the world, or you can cheat people and buy drugs. Yet it's not money that makes you do one thing or the other. The choice is yours.

> **GORILLA MINDSET SHIFT:** WHEN IT COMES TO MONEY, IT'S NOT WHAT YOU MAKE. IT'S WHAT YOU MAKE AND WHAT YOU SAVE.

There are Two Components to Acquiring Wealth – Making Money and Saving Money:

When doing research for what would be a breakthrough book, *The Millionaire Next Door*, the authors learned some startling facts. Most of those we think of as rich really aren't, and often those we view as being of modest means are rich.

The authors of *Millionaire Next Door* learned a secret about many plastic surgeons, doctors, and investment bankers. Not only were they not rich, they were deeply in debt. High-income earners often spend all that they make and then some. When we make more money, we tend to spend more money. There seems to be a habit of growing into our larger incomes. What is going on?

> **GORILLA MINDSET SHIFT:** STOP ATTEMPTING TO BUY YOUR DESIRED STATUS.

The Single Best Way to Save Money:

I am far from a minimalist. I own the newest Macbook, have the best headphones (three different pair actually, as I'm an audiophile), and a top-quality microphone for my podcast. When a new iPhone is released, I buy it, as much of my writing requires original photographs, and the iPhone takes great pics. But I also have a pro-level camera.

I don't buy these items to impress other people. I buy them because they enhance my life, or in the case of my laptop, increase my income.

For a great example of how we often use money to attempt to buy status, look at Beats by Dre. By all objective measures, they are inferior headphones. I have the Sennheiser HD280, Audio-Technica MTX-150, and V-MODA Crossfade 100. All three of those headphones offer better sound quality and noise isolation than Beats by Dre.

A pair of Beats by Dre cost more than the above superior headphones and yet the company Beats is worth more than each of those companies. People purchase Beats for the status. It's not about the audio quality; it's about the logo and message it sends– "I can afford expensive headphones so I'm hip and cool."

Make no mistake, People will judge you by how you dress, and looking professional is important. Yet people often serve as walking billboards for another product. I do not wear clothing with any label on it except my own *Gorilla Mindset* apparel.

Before buying something, ask yourself if the product will enhance your life. Are you buying the product for you, or to impress other people?

Using Money as Medication:

Do you spend money mindlessly? As comedian George Carlin said, do you need more money to buy things you don't need, to impress people you don't like? Do you wear a fancy suit or expensive watch because of what they symbolize? Do you need to dress a certain way to feel valid? Where did those feelings come from? Are those fake needs that other people put inside our heads?

Think about how many people work in jobs they hate. When the paycheck arrives, they spend all of it and often them some, thanks to credit cards. Have you ever heard yourself say this, "What's the point of earning it if I can't spend it?" Perhaps you are using money as a drug to self-medicate and fill a void of an unfulfilling job or home life.

Perhaps your consumerism acts as an opiate for a life void of meaning. Is money the real opiate of the masses?

> **GORILLA MINDSET SHIFT:** DO YOU NEED MORE MONEY OR DO YOU THINK YOU NEED MONEY TO ESCAPE YOUR CURRENT SITUATION?

I am not attacking money. To the contrary, I love money and hope to make a lot more of it every year. Money is great and you should go make as much money as you possibly can — and then some! The question, of course, is how much money do you really want? That's where the mindset shift comes in.

How Can You Make More Money:

Talk about a huge question! While no one has the exact answer for you, as your situation is unique, there are some general mindset shifts you can make. You should start with the most fundamental and important mindset shift that all successful entrepreneurs make — adopt the abundance money mindset.

> **GORILLA MINDSET SHIFT:** YOU SEE MONEY EVERYWHERE. YOU LIVE IN A HUGE WORLD OF ABUNDANT RESOURCES. YOU SEE WEALTH EVERYWHERE.

Think Like a Producer Rather Than a Consumer:

Have you ever purchased a good or service? Sure, you have. Everyone reading this book is a consumer. After all, you did buy this book. You have always thought about things from a consumer perspective. Think about them from a producer's perspective.

Why did you buy that item or service? What drew you into the storefront or onto the website? Why did you click "Buy Now"? Heck, why did you buy *Gorilla Mindset*?

Ask yourself, "Why can't I do what they are doing? Mike just sold me a book. Why can't I sell a book to Mike or someone else?"

You can! Whenever you are out shopping or about to make an online purchase, reflect on what processes led you to become a customer. Then recreate those methods in your own businesses.

Become a Master Middleman:

Although "middlemen" have a bad reputation, a good middleman brings real value to a transaction by bringing together buyers and sellers who might not otherwise have met. Start thinking like a middleman.

For example, one of my businesses is affiliate marketing. I write product and book reviews. When someone buys a product after reading my review, I'm paid what's known as an affiliate commission.

Ultimately, I'm a middleman!

I bring value to buyers and sellers, as my insights into a product are often what persuade a buyer to purchase a product. Without me, the seller would never have sold their product, and the buyer wouldn't have bought a life-enhancing product.

I even have middlemen working for me. My books on green juicing offer a 50% affiliate commission. When someone reviews *Juice Power* or *Fit Juice*, and their review persuades someone to buy my books, the reviewer is paid a 50% commission.

I'm happy to pay those middlemen! When you recommend a product to someone, you are offering value to the person whose product you are recommending and should be compensated.

> **GORILLA MINDSET SHIFT:** IT'S A LIMITING BELIEF THAT YOU HAVE NOTHING OF VALUE TO SHARE. PEOPLE TURN TO YOU FOR ANSWERS BECAUSE YOU HAVE THEM. START GETTING PAID FOR YOUR GUIDANCE.

Wall Street makes billions putting buyers and sellers together, acting as so-called "market makers." You can do the same thing. If you take a vitamin or nutrition supplement, become the middleman. Become the seller, rather than the buyer.

Start Sharing Your Knowledge:

You have skills that you can share with the world. Even if your skills are niche and apply to less than 1% of the human population, there are billions of people on the Internet. People are thirsty for your knowledge!

Chances are that you're not sharing your information, you are keeping it bottled up inside. Perhaps you share that knowledge via word-of-mouth with a friend.

Not sharing your knowledge is a major Gorilla Mindset money making mistake. A friend of mine gives seminars on how to organize your Gmail. It's a great seminar that helps many people who struggle with email organization, and in 60 minutes he can solve their problems.

He has never recorded himself giving this presentation. By recording the conversation, he could share his knowledge. He could sell it, offer it to new clients or upload it to YouTube as a way to market himself.

Even if you're not in tech, you can network your business. Are you a guy in Miami who cuts shrubs? You can use the Internet to drive more business to your brick-and-mortar company.

You may not understand SEO (search engine optimization), and I know the Internet can feel intimidating, but it doesn't have to be that way. Here's a 30 second SEO lesson that others charge thousands for:

- Film some videos of you or your employees cutting shrubs.
- Title it [your city] + [whatever it is you are doing]. What weeds are prevalent in your area? For example: "How to Pull / Kill Bluegrass in North Dakota," or "How to cut down vines in Miami."

Title it based on the specific problem is solves. Is your product the tastiest, lowest in carbohydrates, purely organic, or most sustainable? If you have an ice cream store, start filming videos about the ice cream with the most buttermilk content in the Bronx. Maybe you have the best salted-caramel ice cream in San Francisco. Tell the world!

Do you make the best carrot juice in Venice Beach, California? Give them a video tour of your juice bar.

People are searching on Google for solutions to problems. Remember that Gorilla Mindset Shift you just made? You have solutions to problems, and Google will put you in touch with these people.

People will search for this information, find you, and realize it's easier to hire you. Or maybe they will refer a friend to you. Either way, how long did it take you to share your knowledge? You can download the YouTube app to your phone, film, and upload in minutes.

Even if you're a lawyer, you can share your knowledge. I built up two highly successful law blogs. I worked on a very niche area of law — civil rights litigation, especially excessive force. Whenever I'd perform legal research for a client, I'd file that research away, then I'd take out any identifying information about the client and rewrite the legal briefs into blog posts.

Lawyers and clients who would search Google for specific words — known in law as "terms of art" or "black letter law" — would find my website.

Lawyers and doctors can also film themselves answering common questions. Keep track of frequently asked questions, then film yourself answering them.

In these videos, you can differentiate yourself from all other doctors by showcasing your speaking abilities, body language, and other "bed side manner" skills.

People love putting a face to the name. You can do this easily by filming.

> **GORILLA MINDSET SHIFT:** RECORD EVERYTHING YOU DO. IF YOU HAVE A SMARTPHONE, YOUR VIDEO CAMERA IS HIGHER QUALITY THAN FILM STUDIOS IN THE 1960S. ALL OF THOSE SITCOMS YOU GREW UP WATCHING CAN'T COMPETE WITH YOUR TECHNOLOGY.

Skate to Where the Puck Is Going:

Wayne Gretzky is the greatest hockey player who ever lived. Some say Michael Jordan was the Wayne Gretzky of basketball.

When asked why he was such an amazing hockey player, Gretzky replied, "A good hockey player plays where the puck is. A *great* hockey player plays where the puck is going to be."

Get to the market before it's a market. For example, have you noticed that there is a juice bar on nearly every street corner? In some parts of New York, San Francisco, and Los Angeles, juice bars are as common as Starbucks.

The juice market resurged after Joe Cross released a documentary about his weight loss and health transformation called *Fat, Sick, and Nearly Dead*. When his documentary was released, many people saw economic opportunity.

Just over three years ago, people skated to where the juicing market was going. *Fat, Sick, and Nearly Dead* launched a billion-dollar juicing industry. I joined that business. When I saw Joe Cross's movie, I knew juicing would be big. I started my own websites about juicing, and then even wrote a juicing book that has sold more than many best sellers.

Where is the market heading? Have you seen a movie or advertisement lately and noticed a new trend? Perhaps what you *haven't* seen evidences a great trend.

Nike, Dove, and every other large corporation, has chosen to put women first. Although advancing women's interests is laudable, men are being neglected.

The corporate message is that, "Men are alone," and, "Men must look out for themselves." Men are a largely neglected market segment. Yes, there are companies selling juvenile stupidity to males, but *men* are a neglected market.

GQ recently hired a former staff writer from a notorious anti-male website. What was once a magazine for gentlemen has now taken a decidedly anti-male tone. There are few sources of information for mature men. Indeed, one reason my websites have grown is because I'm not afraid to stick up for men. Yes, it is possible to advance the causes of men without being anti-women. After all, men are fathers to daughters, husbands to wives, sons to mothers and brothers to sisters.

Find a way to serve men, both young and old. Position yourself as a leader in what will be an exploding market.

Become a Trusted Authority:

We've been taught that only certain people are authorities. You need a white lab coat or a degree. That's nonsense. It's a social construct created to make you sheep rather than wolves. Many of you blindly trust the authorities rather than become an authority yourself.

GORILLA MINDSET SHIFT: BECOME A TRUSTED AUTHORITY.

If you have the answer to a problem, you are an authority on that problem. Now you have to become a *trusted* authority. You have to build trust. To build trust, follow the rule that all writers have laser beamed into their foreheads: "Show, don't tell."

Don't tell people you're an expert. Show them. That's where those YouTube videos will come in handy. If you lost 20 pounds of fat, post your before and after pictures, and your food and exercise diary. You're not telling them you're an expert on fat loss, you're showing them.

The Halo Effect:

When you establish yourself as a trusted authority in any area, people will believe you have the answers to other problems. This is due to the halo effect.

The halo effect is a well-recognized heuristic, or thinking shortcut we take. If someone shows is expertise on one subject, we assume (rightly or wrongly) that he's an expert on every other subject.

Often this backfires. For example, Neil DeGrasse Tyson is an authority on astrophysics, but when he talks about politics, he seems sort of dopey, yet the halo effect still holds. Someone who is an authority in one area must screw up pretty badly in another area before he will be discredited.

To create a halo around you, exercise professionalism in all you do. Show that you are an authority every day. When people ask you questions, give well-researched, solid answers. Admit when you don't know something.

Be transparent. Even when people catch you making a mistake, embrace it. Thank them. Remember the reframing techniques, "I am so transparent because this is how we all grow together."

Once you have created a halo effect for yourself, do not abuse this trust. Your status as a trusted authority can be destroyed overnight.

Remember, there is always someone out there willing to throw you under the bus, so be honest, forthright and transparent in all you do.

As Warren Buffett said, "It takes a lifetime to build a reputation and 20 seconds to destroy one. If you go through life with that mindset, you'll do things differently."

Also, remember that transparency will help you more than hurt you. I can't be caught doing anything because I've disclosed everything.

Even if I made a mistake and someone tried to ruin my reputation, I could defend myself easily. Maybe I left something out unintentionally, but because I have built truth through transparency, people would believe me, rather than assume the worst.

We're all human. We mess up and make mistakes, we're not infallible. But when you've established yourself as a trusted authority, forgiveness will come quickly if you admit your mistakes, so long as you aren't deliberately committing fraud or abusing people's trust.

This chapter could be hundreds of pages longer, but making money is easy once you adopt the right mindset. Now that your head is in the right place, you will see opportunity everywhere. You now live in a world of abundance and are willing to take action.

Use these Gorilla Mindset Shift affirmations as a reminder:

- I have solved problems that others struggle with. Therefore, I have the answers that others need.
- I am a content creator.
- If I want to be a TV star, I'll start a YouTube Channel. If I want to be a radio star, I'll start a podcast. If I want to become a writer, I'll publish my own books.
- I am a producer and not a consumer.
- My reputation is everything. I will never abuse the trust others instill in me.

Once you make those Gorilla Mindset Shifts, you'll start seeing money and opportunity everywhere.

Investing Your Money:

Now that you're on your way to making and saving money, a natural question arises: "Where do I put my money?" Before deciding, do the following:

- have an emergency cash savings of 6–12 months in living expenses
- pay off your credit cards
- begin to dollar-cost average (I will explain this term shortly) into the market at regular intervals.

After that, you should invest intelligently.

How I invest comes directly from Wall Street insiders, including Europe's Hedge Fund Manager of the Decade, and financial advisers at America's largest investment banks.

GORILLA MINDSET SHIFT: BECOME AN INVESTOR, NOT A TRADER.

What I am about to say will outrage many people (primarily men, as men seem to have a belief they are expert day traders), yet this advice has been echoed by the richest men in the world, including Warren Buffett. Unless you have an edge (that is, some inside information or insight no one else has), you should not trade in the stock market. Warren Buffett has beaten the market year after year. Upon his death, his wealth will go to low-cost mutual funds.

When I wrote before about why men should be investors, not traders, hundreds wrote in to tell me I'm crazy! They have all beaten the market, they told me. I'm sure you also know someone who always has some hot stock tip. Everyone claims they are day traders, and it seems to be a phase most men go through. Yet if those men are earning such high returns, why aren't they running hedge funds with other people's money? That is far more profitable than day trading. It doesn't add up.

Most men don't show you all their trades. In fact, one Internet marketer who claimed to have turned a 10K investment into millions of dollars has refused to allow an audit of his account. Be wary of people who claim to be day traders, or who only talk about their one or two big scores. Look at how they perform over a ten-year period.

Dollar-Cost Averaging:

Dollar-cost averaging into the market means you buy low-cost mutual funds at regular intervals. You do not try to time the market. Rather than wait until someone else tells you, "NOW is the time you buy," you purchase index funds at regular intervals.

For example, I purchase low-cost index funds with Vanguard every 3 months. This is done like clockwork. I don't wait to buy if I think the market is going to rise or fall. I exercise discipline. Some people dollar-cost average into the market monthly. One problem with this approach is buying funds has a transaction cost. (With Fidelity, it's around $8.95.) Those costs can eat into your long-term gains, especially if you're not investing large amounts of money at one time.

Low-Cost Index Funds:

Just like the name, a low-cost index fund is an index fund with low costs. Costs are hidden inside most mutual funds, and the impact, even a seemingly low one percent, can have on your overall market return is staggering. An index fund tracks the overall performance of the stock market. If you believe, as I do, that cost of living is only going to increase, then you believe companies selling the stuff you need will also increase in value.

The S&P 500 is comprised of the biggest 500 stocks, and is a bellwether of the overall stock market.

Hence my approach is to invest in a low-cost index fund. I invest in SPY and FDI every three months. Those funds do not have any hidden fees.

GORILLA MINDSET SHIFT: DOLLAR-COST AVERAGING TAKES DISCIPLINE, WHICH YOU HAVE AN ABUNDANCE OF.

That's a summary of my investing strategy. It's not glamorous, it takes discipline, and it's sort of boring, but I realize investing in the stock market is not a short-term play to get me rich. To get rich, you must invest in the most important stock out there — You, Inc.

You, Inc.:

If you talk to some real Wall Street players about investing, they'll all ask you the same question, "What is your edge?" Your "edge" is the information (sometimes insider information, sometimes perfectly legally obtainable information) you have that no one else has. What do you know about a stock? There is a stock so valuable and unique that no one else except you can buy it.

> **GORILLA MINDSET SHIFT:** YOU HAVE AN EDGE IN THE MOST-VALUABLE STOCK OUT THERE — YOU, INC.

When it comes to making money, how do you see yourself? Do you see yourself as a laborer, a worker, a drone, or a wage slave? There is no wrong answer here. If you have low feelings of self-worth, as you have seen in chapter after chapter, those can be changed by reframing and controlling your mental state.

I view myself as a corporation. I am the most valuable stock in the world, because there is only one of me. When you see yourself as a corporation, you begin making fundamental changes in your behavior. As we discussed previously, you begin seeing yourself as a producer rather than a consumer. You begin looking for ways to add value to transactions, and indeed, you are now looking for ways to get in between transactions. You're becoming the middle man.

You also take concrete steps to improve your life. Purchasing *Gorilla Mindset* proves that you are willing to invest in yourself. Just as a corporation buys new equipment and hires employees to increase its bottom line, you educate yourself and begin seeing yourself as your own personal brand.

You, Inc. Is Your Unique Personal Brand:

When you seek "face time with the higher ups," you're recognizing you have a brand. You want to get noticed. That "face time" implies they'll recognize your achievements. Yet, you often realize being recognized doesn't get you very far, and you are not sure why. Perhaps your "face" isn't all that different from everyone else's. Perhaps you aren't unique. Begin thinking of ways to distinguish yourself from the rest of the people in your office or workplace. They are generics. You are your own brand.

For example, "*Mike Cernovich*" is a brand, "*Cernovich.com*," is a website I run, and each have their own trademark. *Gorilla Mindset* is also a trademarked brand. While my message may not be suitable for the masses of men and women who live lives of hopelessness and despair, I do have a message. My message is one of unapologetic self-development. I don't apologize for seeking to better my life and I do not expect you to make any apologies for your life either.

You don't need to be an author or public speaker to think of yourself as having your own brand.

Differentiation:

Why do you choose Coke over Pepsi or use a Mac rather than a PC? Are you reading *Gorilla Mindset* on a Kindle, iPhone, or iPad, or listening to it?

You choose your preference from the product differences that meet your needs or tastes. You drink Coke because it tastes different from Pepsi, and read your books on a Kindle because the font appears different than it does on an iPhone. You are different from everyone else in your office. How? Look around. Do you do work no one else can or will? Do you show up earlier and stay later than everyone else? Does your work stand out or blend in?

To become your own recognizable personal brand — You, Inc. — you must find a way to differentiate yourself. Being different is not without challenges. We are taught from birth to conform to the expectations of others — be it from our parents, teachers, or society in general. Differentiation requires you to be unique and unapologetically you.

Get Used to Being Rejected:

When you develop your own personal brand by differentiating yourself from the rest of the pack, it stands to reason that some people will love you. However, some people will always hate you, as society often dislikes those who have the courage to stand up and be recognized. Fortunately, you have the mindset techniques to deal with the haters. You are a master of self-talk, reframing, and mindfulness. Hate and negative criticism no longer have any power over you.

Choose Yourself:

One of my favorite books is *Choose Yourself* by James Altucher. *Choose Yourself* is a raw look at today's economy. Large companies are looking for ways to cut costs, which translates into ways to fire you, decrease your benefits, and expect you to do more for less. In *Choose Yourself*, Altucher makes the compelling case that the days of doing good work and being discovered are long over. Instead of waiting to be discovered, you must choose yourself.

For example, I wanted to start a podcast. No one asked me to be a guest on their show. I chose myself by starting a podcast, which is now the highest-rated mindset podcast on iTunes. When I wanted to write a book on mindset, I didn't wait for a publishing house to approach me. Instead, I chose myself by self-publishing *Gorilla Mindset*.

After choosing myself by crowd-funding a movie, I was even able to meet James Altucher, who graciously agreed to appear in my documentary on free speech – *Silenced*.

Find ways to choose yourself in your own life. Ask yourself, are you waiting for others to recognize and appreciate you? Take action. Become your own hype man and marketing and PR department. If you have a goal or desire, stop waiting around for others to give you the chance. Seize the opportunity by choosing yourself.

Tax Planning:

Even if you have a job, you can start a side business to enjoy immense tax advantages. Tax planning is as important as investing in the stock market. (Note: This is not legal advice, and the specifics of this section apply to readers in the United States, but the mindset shifts are the same. Look for ways to minimize your tax bill.)

> **GORILLA MINDSET SHIFT:** PLAN AHEAD FOR YOUR FINANCIAL FUTURE BY MINIMIZING YOUR TAX BILL TODAY.

The High Costs of Paying Taxes:

Paying taxes today will leave you with substantially less money tomorrow. Your total returns will decrease, as compounding will not be amplified due to the smaller amount of money you're investing.

For example:

- $10,000 compounded on a yearly basis over the course of 30 years at a 5% interest rate would be worth: $43,219.
- $7,500 compounded on a yearly basis over the course of 30 years at a 5% interest rate would be worth: $32,415.

In other words, that $2,500 you lose to the tax man today is $11,000 less money you will have tomorrow. More pre-tax dollars invested today means more money compounding, and thus, more money at retirement.

Self-Employment Tax Tips:

To save the most on your taxes, you need to become self-employed. It's possible to become self-employed even while working at a regular, salaried job. Many successful workers and employees operate businesses on the side.

Who is self-employed? If you're in the United States, the only answer that matters comes from the Internal Revenue Service:

> *Generally, you are self-employed if any of the following apply to you:*
>
> - *You carry on a trade or business as a sole proprietor or an independent contractor.*
> - *You are a member of a partnership that carries on a trade or business.*
> - *You are otherwise in business for yourself (including a part-time business).*
> - *In other words, you're self-employed if you run a business.*

Are You Considered Self-Employed if You Have A Normal Job:

Yes, as the IRS notes, you can run a business full or part time. Many stay-at-home mothers sell products from home, which is a legitimate business enterprise. For example, after working at your normal job you could start up a website and affiliate-market books and other products.

Beware of the Hobby Loss Rule:

If you're going to treat your blog like a business for tax purposes, then be prepared to prove to the IRS you are running the blog as a business rather than a hobby. The hobby loss rule tends to get triggered when people become "too creative" when claiming to run a business. For example, sometimes people start a travel website and then begin deducting vacation expenses, which is something the IRS tends to frown upon.

Tax-Deductible Business Expenses:

Per the IRS:

> *To be deductible, a business expense must be both ordinary and necessary. An ordinary expense is one that is common and accepted in your trade or business. A necessary expense is one that is helpful and appropriate for your trade or business. An expense does not have to be indispensable to be considered necessary.*

That seems a bit circular, so think of it like this: If you need to spend money to run your business, then it's a business expense. Here's some examples of general business expenses:

- The mileage on your car from business travel.
- If you use a dedicated part of your home for an office, you may deduct this as a home-office business expense.
- It costs money to wine and dine clients, hence meals and entertainment can be deducted from your tax bill.
- Travel to and from a work site.

This list of deductible business expenses is not intended to be exhaustive. Again, you are changing your mindset about money by thinking of ways to minimize your tax bill, but always hire an accountant!

Business Expenses for Professional Content Creators Example:

In my line of work, I incur a lot of business expenses. Since I work 100% online writing, speaking, and traveling, these are some expenses I write off on my tax bill:

- MacBook Pro
- Microphone for podcasts
- SoundCloud subscriptions
- iPhone bill
- Hosting/server/Host Gator/Cloudflare fees
- Web design/logo design
- Email newsletter service/MailChimp/aWeber
- Themes for blog
- Books that I review on Cernovich.com
- Camera for D&P pictures and YouTube
- Products I buy to review

As you can see, there are many tax benefits to running your own business. Yes, you can earn a living (as I do) or earn some spare cash (as others do) while blogging. You can also save on your tax bill.

Retirement Planning for the Self-Employed:

You can pay taxes today or you can pay taxes tomorrow, but you will pay taxes. You can pay taxes before contributing to a retirement account like a 401(k) or IRA, or you can pay taxes tomorrow when you withdraw the money.

Is it better to pay your taxes before contributing to your IRA, or after? Generally speaking, it's better to defer your tax payments so that your contributions to your retirement account can benefit from the law of compounding interest.

SEP 401(k)/Self-Employed 401(k)/Uni-(k):

A SEP 401(k) is a retirement account available to self-employed people. Again, we look to the IRS for guidance:

> *Simplified Employee Pension (SEP) Contribute as much as 25% of your net earnings from self-employment (not including contributions for yourself), up to $52,000 for 2014 ($53,000 for 2015).*

With a SEP 401(k), you stash away pre-tax income to benefit from the law of compounding interest. You don't pay taxes until you withdraw your money, decades later. In other words, your money grows tax free. The $10,000 you put into an SEP will be worth considerably more than it would have been had you contributed $7,500 in after-tax income.

Should You Open a Roth 401(k) or a SEP 401(k):

With a Roth 401(k), you pay your income taxes today. You do not pay taxes when you make withdrawals from your IRA, sometime in the future. Wait, won't you miss out on the law of compound interest by funding a Roth IRA? If you will earn more in the future (and thus be taxed at a higher rate) than you earn today, it may make more sense to pay your taxes today.

Again, talk to your tax advisor or continue your education. There's no way to explain what investments will work best for you. This is something you need to start taking seriously, however, as the implications are massive.

How to Open a Self-Employed 401(k):

Fidelity, Schwab, and Vanguard are all low-cost brokerage firms with sterling reputations. They also provide a wealth of material to help you decide what accounts to open and how to invest.

For more information on tax planning, go to GorillaMindset.com/Money for links to additional resources.

GORILLA MONEY HABITS

View Yourself as an Investment:

You are a company — You, Inc. Invest in your company. Learn about your company. Study it with the most intense detail. Eating healthy foods will save you healthcare costs in the long run. Reading books will help you improve your life and keep your mind sharp. In fact, reading can help delay, mitigate, and prevent many forms of early-onset dementia.

If You Use Credit, Do it Wisely:

If you can't afford to buy it, don't buy it. This seems like a simple tip, and yet so often credit card companies offer incentives like free travel to entice you into signing up for a credit card. If you use credit cards, pay off the balance in full each month.

Start a Side Business for Tax Deductions:

Part of the Gorilla Mindset Shift is to see yourself as a producer rather than a consumer. Once you start your own business, even if it's only a side business, you are well on your way to earning more money.

Start Saving for Retirement Today:

Dollar-cost average into the stock market every month. Do not become a day trader. Be an investor, and invest for the long term. Keep buying. Sometimes you'll buy high and sometimes you'll buy low.

Differentiate Between Wants and Needs:

When you're broke, you don't get to buy what you want. You only get to buy what you need. Never delude yourself into believing a want is a need.

If You Get a Raise, Live Off Your Old Salary:

You were living just fine off your old salary. Do not grow into it. Instead, save the increase or put that money towards a side business.

If You Receive a Large Sum, Don't Spend it for a Year:

Maybe you'll receive a huge bonus at work, an inheritance, or even win the lottery. Do not spend the money for a year or else you'll end up like so many lottery winners — broke.

CHAPTER 10

Mindset and Vision: Change What You See, Change What You Get

Visualization has been used for centuries by athletes to improve their performance. You can use the same visualization techniques in your own life, and in fact, you probably already are and don't realize it.

The Power of Visualization:

In a famous study, basketball players who wanted to improve free throw performance were asked to do one of the following:

a) shoot 100 free throws a day

b) do not shoot any free throws, just visualize yourself throwing them

c) shoot 100 free throws and perform the visualization exercises

To the shock of researchers, those athletes who shot 100 free throws improved the least. Yes, you read that correctly: Those who visualized shooting free throws improved more than those who practiced them. And those who used both visualization exercises and physical practice improved the most.

GORILLA MINDSET SHIFT: YOU MAY THINK VISUALIZATION IS DIFFICULT. IN TRUTH, YOU HAVE ALREADY MASTERED VISUALIZATION.

You may believe visualization is challenging, but in fact, you have already mastered it:

- Do you think about the past or ponder bad memories?
- When you think about the past, do you involve one or more of your five senses (sight, sound, taste, touch, smell)?
- Do you feel happy or sad when you think about the past?
- Does thinking about the past elicit emotions in you? That is, does your mood or mental state change?

Thinking about the past is nothing more than performing a visualization exercise.

How to Begin Consciously Using Visualization:

Start by applying all of your senses. Again, you already know how to visualize. Thinking about and reflecting on the past is a form of visualization. When you think about the past, do you feel the moment? Sometimes you can even hear the sounds and see the sights of the memory. It's like you're really there. Rather than ponder the past, visualize your future. Think of a goal you'd like to achieve. Maybe it's making more money, finding a better job or getting fit.

Imagine yourself achieving that goal. Think about where you will be sitting when you reach your goal. What will you look and feel like? Will you be sitting in a large leather chair behind a thick oak desk, or maybe on a hammock in a tropical paradise?

Your visualization must be specific. The difference between visualization and daydreaming is this: Visualization is specific and targeted towards a goal. When you visualize, you will see how the prior *Gorilla Mindset* techniques come into play. As you begin visualizing where you want to be and who you want to be with, your mental state will change. You'll begin feeling stronger, more powerful, and triumphant. Then you will carry that with you and channel it when life is hard.

Your Dreams Are More Realistic Than Your Memories:

What if you started from the proposition that your past does not exist? What if you treated memories as no more real than imagination? That view is not too far off base. There's a large body of cognitive science showing that our memories range from horribly biased to outright false.

When you think about sad memories, for example — you develop feelings of sadness, rage, bitterness, resentment, or disempowerment. You feel this way because you choose to treat your memories as if they are real. Make no mistake, that is a choice you make in the present moment. Your memories are real only because you choose to treat them as real.

Look Where You're Going, Not Where You've Been:

For the rest of the day, do not think about the past. When a memory arises, remind yourself, "This is not real." Instead of thinking about the past, visualize the future. Picture what you want. Involve all of your available senses. Visualize your perfect day. Feel this picture-perfect day as being real.

Use those visualization skills that you have wasted on thinking about the past to dream about a better future. You'll be surprised by what and who you attract into your life.

You Must See It to Want It:

I grew up in the heartland of America. Surrounded by corn fields, soy beans, and factories, I had no idea what the ocean was. The ocean was some abstract thing.

I loading up my 1989 red Ford Escort to visit my sister on the East Coast. My dad and I gotten into an argument, as he didn't want me to take the road trip. He wasn't a hater, he was a kind, but small-minded man, who lived in the prison of his own mind.

You see, I grew up dirt poor in a small hick town. I still have a horrible sense of direction and get lost on the freeways.

We never had a family vacation. We couldn't travel more than an hour away from home, because if the old clucker did start, it was likely to break down not far down the road. I watched my dad suffer second degree burns after the car overheated on a highway less than a half hour from home.

Maybe I was delusional. Or maybe all of that "self-help crap" that people mock made me fearless. Either way, I popped Dale Carnegie's *"How to Stop Worrying and Start Living"* into my CD player and set off.

Then my life changed.

After arriving at my sister's house, we went to stay at her father-in-law's ocean property. I had never seen the ocean or stayed in a nice home. The home I grew up in was furnished with couches that better off people were throwing away and there were holes in the carpet. I was always ashamed to bring friends over, and having a girl over was out of the question!

I can still remember hearing the ocean waves crash against the beach. I can still smell the salt water. That's when I told my sister, "I want to be rich."

I knew what I wanted and nothing was going to stop me.

Looking back, it all seems sort of childish — silly even. The apartment was a time share that probably only cost a few grand each year in upkeep fees.

Today I can see the ocean whenever I want. I can drop the top in a fun car that I own, not lease, and cruise up the Pacific Coast Highway.

But it all started in that moment out East, when I heard the waves crashing, smelled the salt water and saw a sea turtle laying eggs at night.

People often ask me how they can find their life purpose or motivation. They don't like my answer, but it's the only one I'm capable of giving:

If you feel unfulfilled, stop what you're doing. Try something else. Walk the streets until you're exhausted. Repeat this every day.

When you finally see what you want, your life will change.

THE VISUALIZATION WORKSHEET

To get the most out of visualization, you must imagine concrete situations. They need to be fact-based, involving all of your available senses.

Where do you want to live in 1, 3, or 5 years? The time frame doesn't matter. What does matter is seeing yourself in the future.

Write it out: _____

Here's an example: I was sitting on my couch in Venice Beach when I started visualizing myself writing out of cafes across the world. Two years later, that's where I am.

Involve all of your available five senses (sight, feeling, taste, touch, smell). If you want to live by the ocean, smell the sea salt. Hear the waves crashing against the beach. See the sea gulls flying overhead. Taste the salt from mist in your tongue. Smell the clean, crisp air.

If you want to develop a better relationship with your friends, family or loved ones, you can also use these visualization exercises. How do you want your spouse, child, or parents to see you? Imagine yourself being that person.

GORILLA VISUALIZATION HABITS

Remind yourself you are already a master of visualization. After all, you can make yourself feel a certain way by thinking of your past. The past is no more real than the future.

Treat your dreams as more real than your memories. When you catch yourself thinking about the past, get into the present moment. Tell yourself, "I am going to imagine myself living in the future."

Finally, take time each day to practice visualization. You won't live your dream life overnight. Take a few minutes each day imagining where you want to be.

CHAPTER 11

MINDSET STARTS TODAY: CREATING YOUR AMAZING LIFE ONE DAY AT A TIME

You now have all of the tools you need to live your life mindfully. You understand mental strategies like self-talk, reframing, mindfulness, and mental state. You are able to change how you think and feel, leading to improvements in your personal and professional lives. You also realize that the mind and body are connected, and that your lifestyle, health, fitness and finances are all connected. It is time to put together everything you have learned.

What you want is an amazing life free from anxiety. You want to feel good. To live an amazing life, you must first start by living an amazing day. Begin visualizing your perfect day in as much detail as you can. If you imagine yourself living by the ocean, hear the sound of the waves and smell the salt water. Daydream, and as you do, recognize that you are getting closer to your dreams becoming reality. You must *see* what you want, to *get* what you want.

My Perfect Day:

We all have different desires, so our perfect day will look different. Here is how I imagine my day to be. Adopt, refine or reject what doesn't fit *your* perfect day:

I wake up excited and ready to get to work. I usually have numerous emails and reader comments to review. I also check to see how many books I sold overnight.

I like my readers. They don't post negative or stupid comments. Their comments edify me and each other. I learn something new from them every day.

I take a contrast shower, perform a brain-warm up, and am ready to begin my day.

I get in the moment, writing 3,000 to 5,000 words about whatever I want. I don't write just to impress people or in hopes of getting massive page views. I stay on my message, seeking to attract like-minded men and women.

When some tech or design issue comes up, it annoys me but I recognize that tech and design is part of being a professional writer, so I embrace the suck for the greater good.

After a few hours of work, I head to the gym for a hard training session. I push my body, but not to the point of exhaustion. I leave with positive feelings. My body feels good and refreshed.

I grab a large green juice and some protein powder to help my body begin the recovery process, after talking to some friends or training partners, I return to work.

Reader questions and comments pour in. I file them away to answer during podcasts or to write about later.

I genuinely want to help people who write in, because as noted above, I liking my readers.

Reader emails and comments keep coming in. I go to bed spent, but not demoralized or dejected.

I fall asleep next to someone I love, knowing that tomorrow will be another day full of opportunity and enrichment.

THE PERFECT DAY WORKSHEET

It helps to write out what you imagine The Perfect Day to be like. The more detail you use, the better. When writing out The Perfect Day, start with the five W's — Who, What, When, Where, and Why.

Who do you wake up next to?

Do you wake up alone? Are you with a man, woman, or maybe the family dog is asleep at your feet.

What do you do after you wake up?

Maybe you pray, meditate, play with your kids.

When do you go to work?

Do you start working immediately in the morning, or get a late start?

Where do you wake up?

Is it in a large city, a small cabin in the woods, or maybe a hammock in Thailand?

Why do you wake up?

Do you wake up because you have to be somewhere, or because you are excited for what the day may hold?

Use as much detail as possible. In fact, you cannot use too much detail when performing this visualization exercise.

WHAT'S NEXT?

If you've made it this far into the book, I hope you've enjoyed it. Hopefully you have the same feeling I get when reading a great book – disappointed that's it's over. While the book has ended, our conversation has only just begun. I write thousands of words each week and have over 100 podcasts for you to listen to.

There are numerous other places we can continue our work together.

You can listen to the Mike Cernovich Podcast on iTunes and Android: soundcloud.com/cernovich

GorillaMindset.com contains links to all of the articles and books mentioned, as well as a free supplement guide for you. Some of the pages are password protected. The password is Cernovich.

Also, since *Gorilla Mindset* is worksheet based, I'm including a free PDF edition. There is no catch, just go to this link to claim your free copy: GorillaMindset.com/pdf

If you enjoyed *Gorilla Mindset*, please give it an honest review on Amazon. It helps others find the powerful message of mindset, allowing them to improve their own lives and the broader world.

Printed in Great Britain
by Amazon